Aunt's Friends

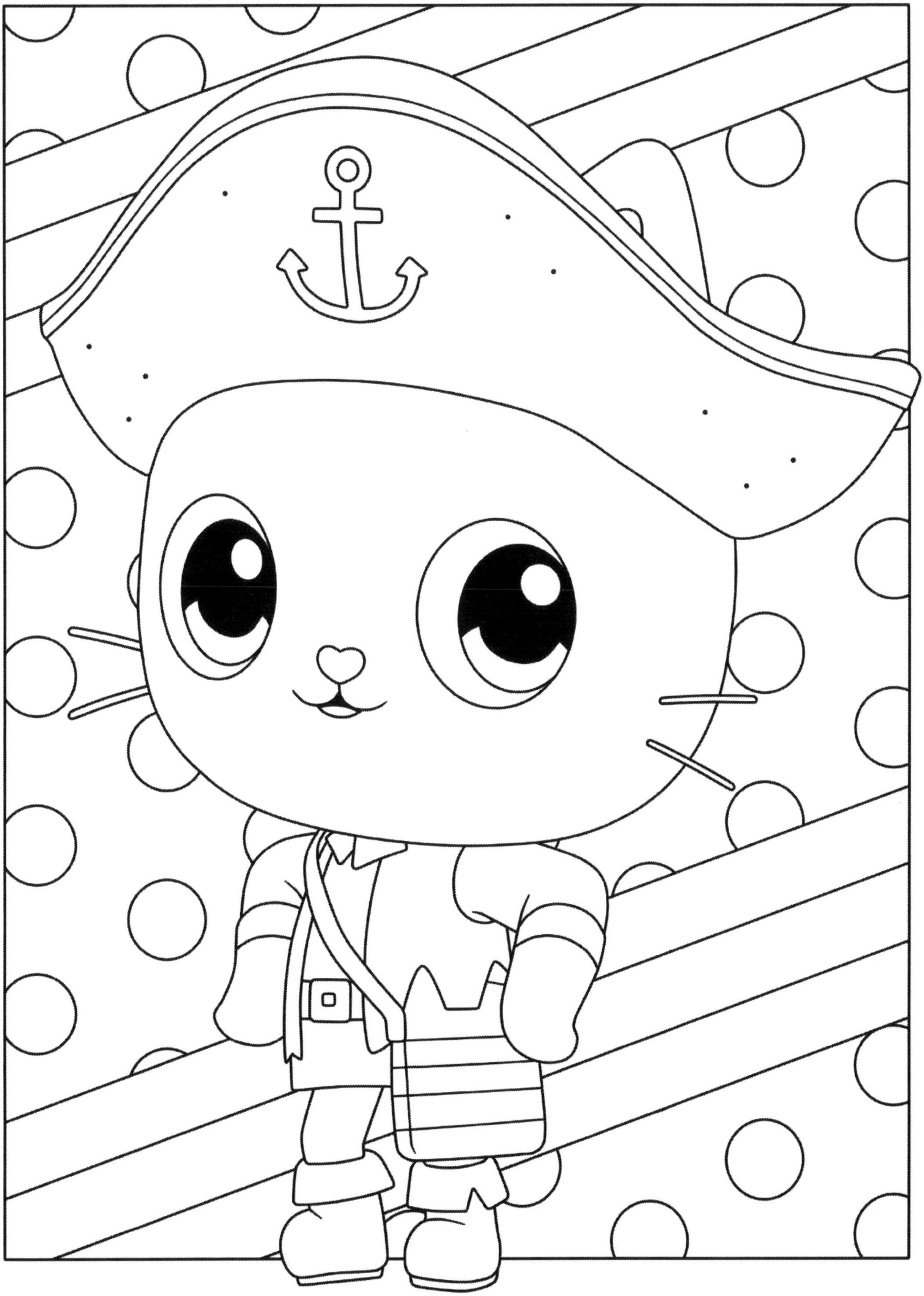

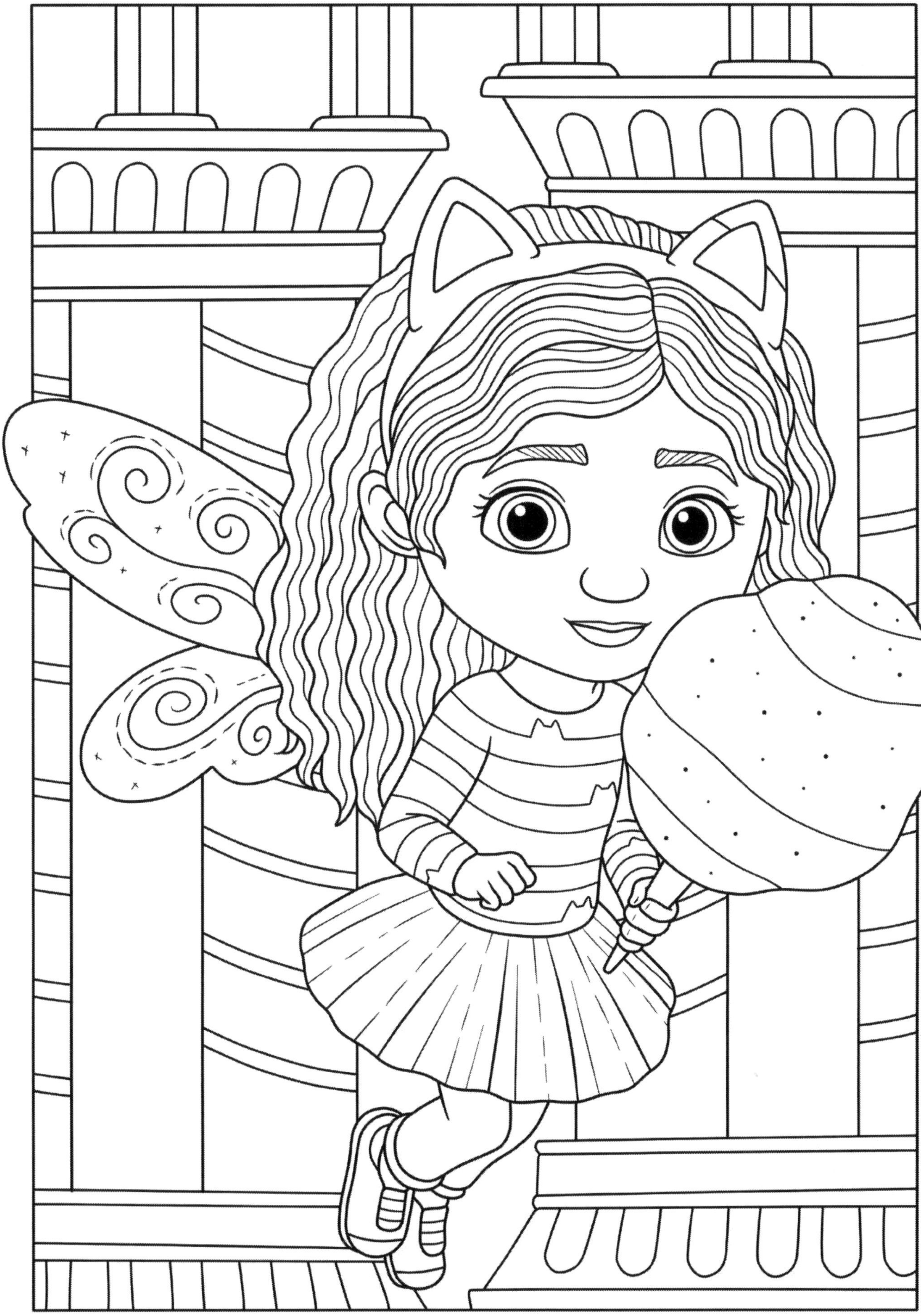

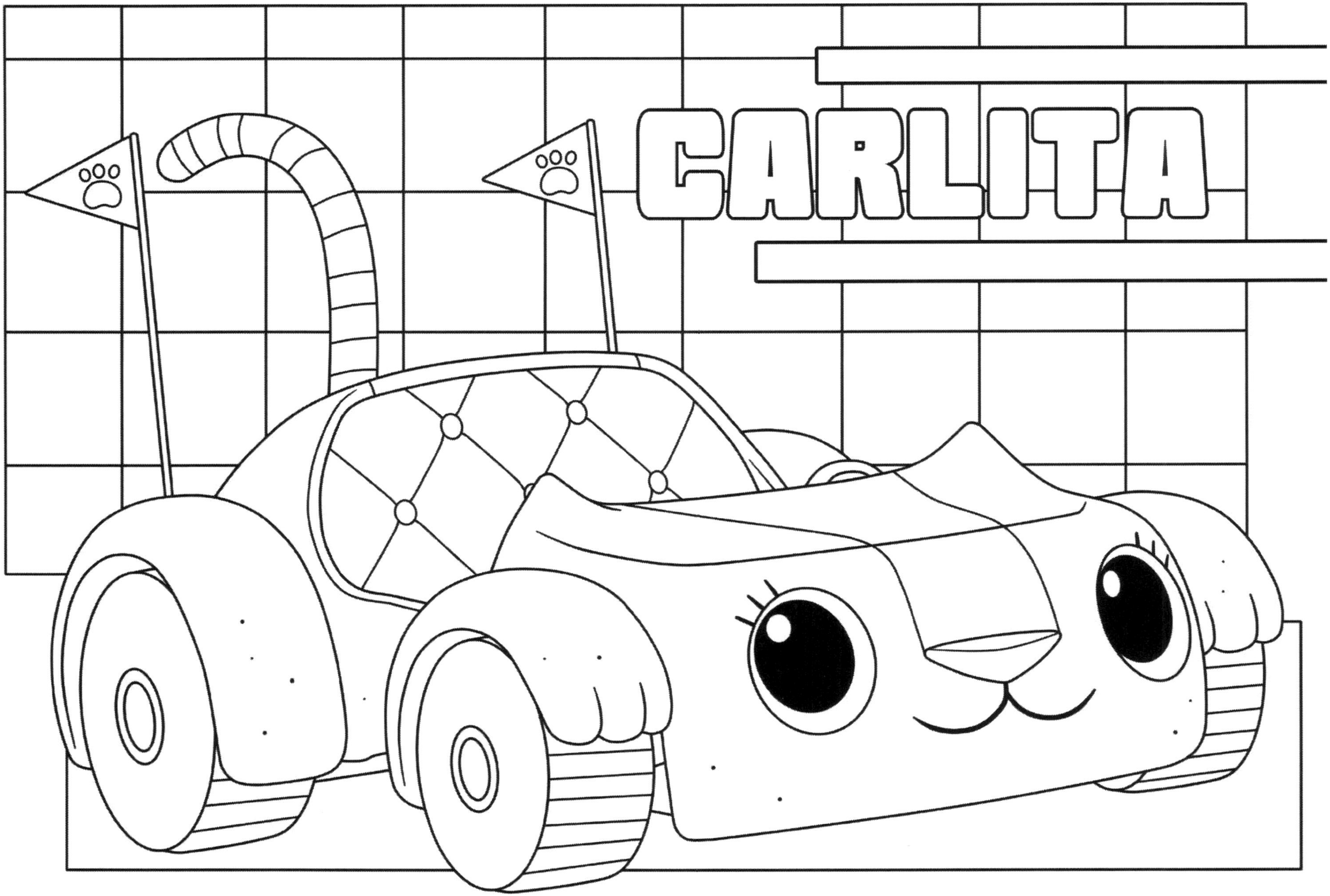
CARLITA

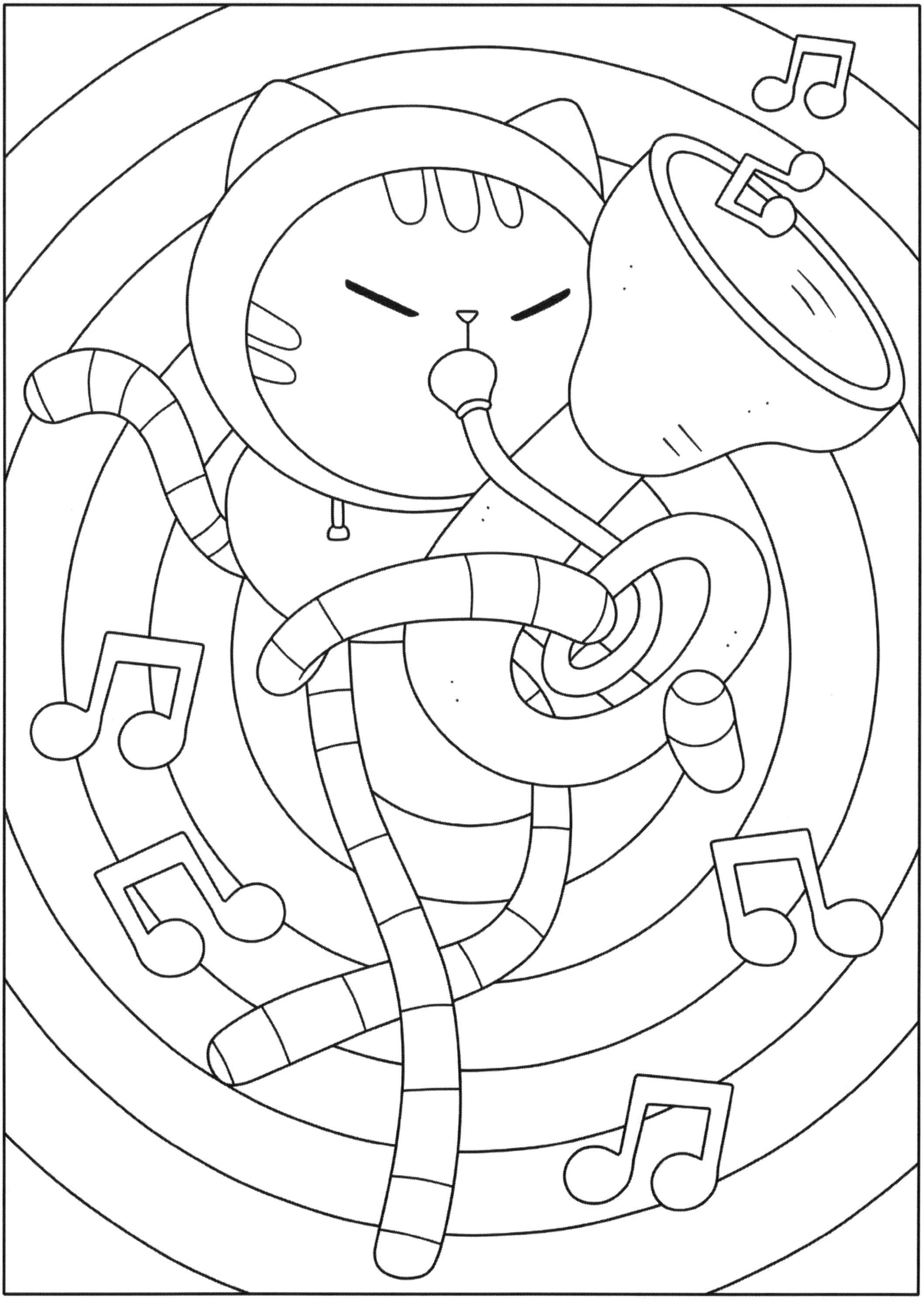

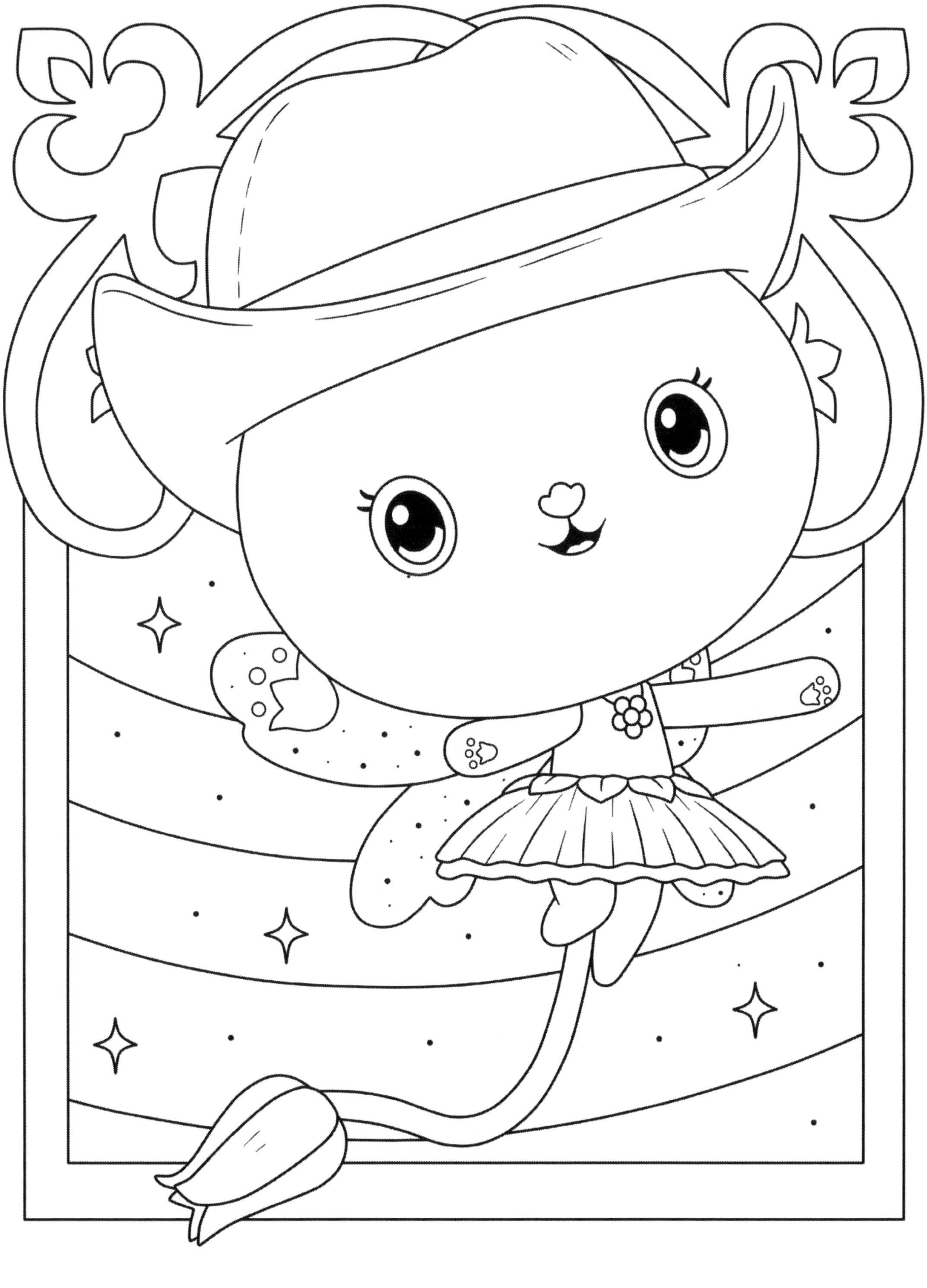

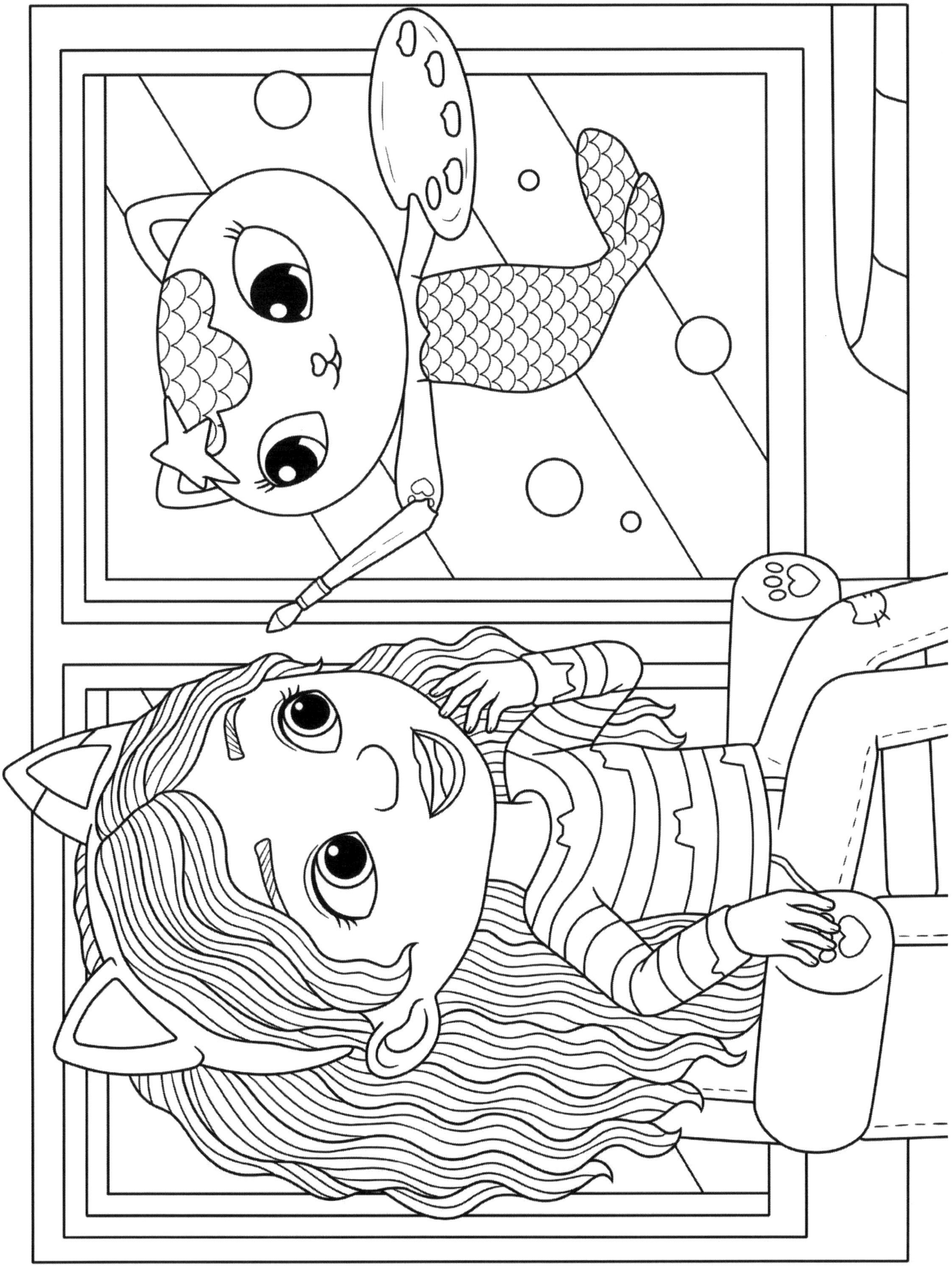

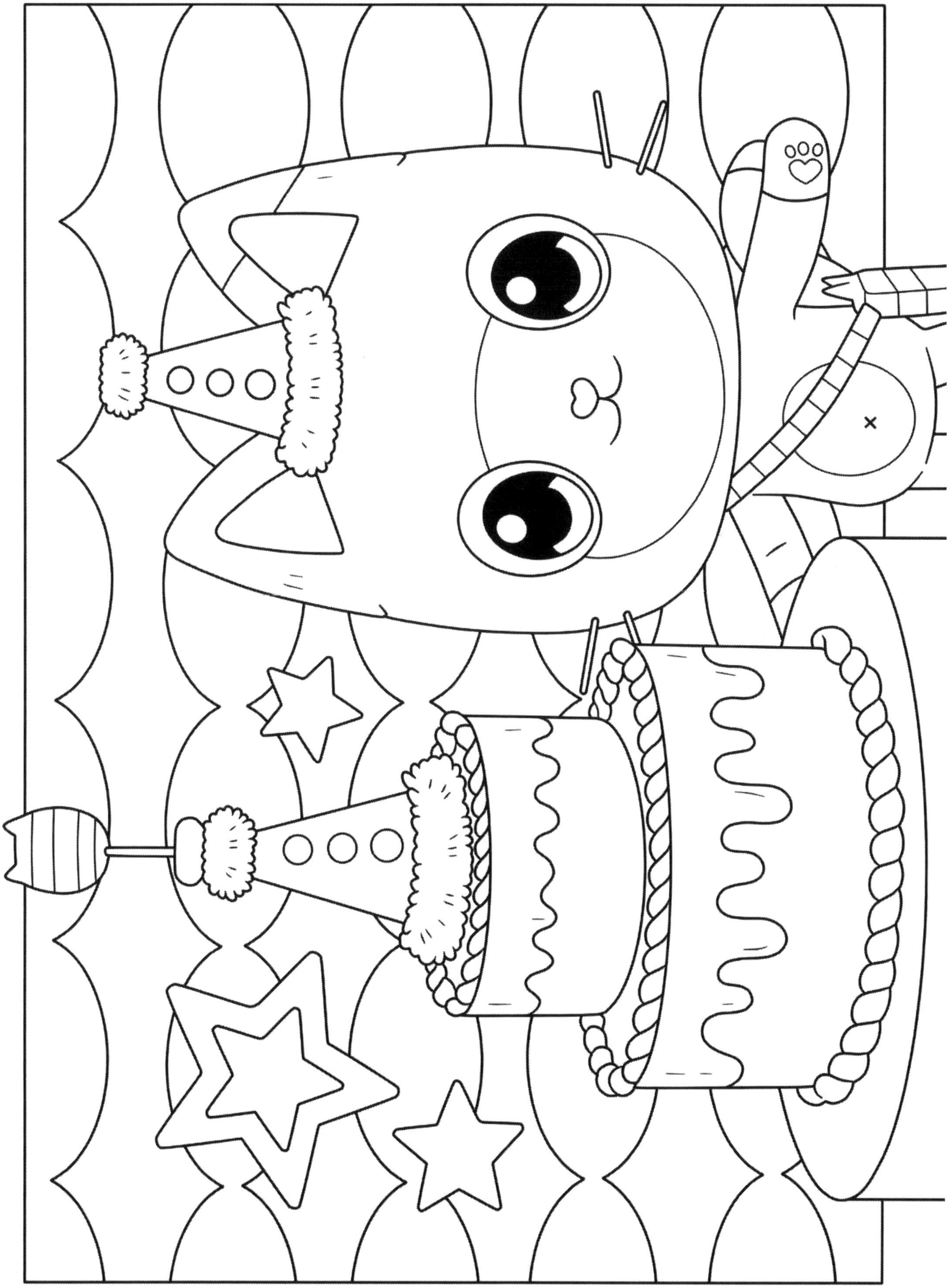

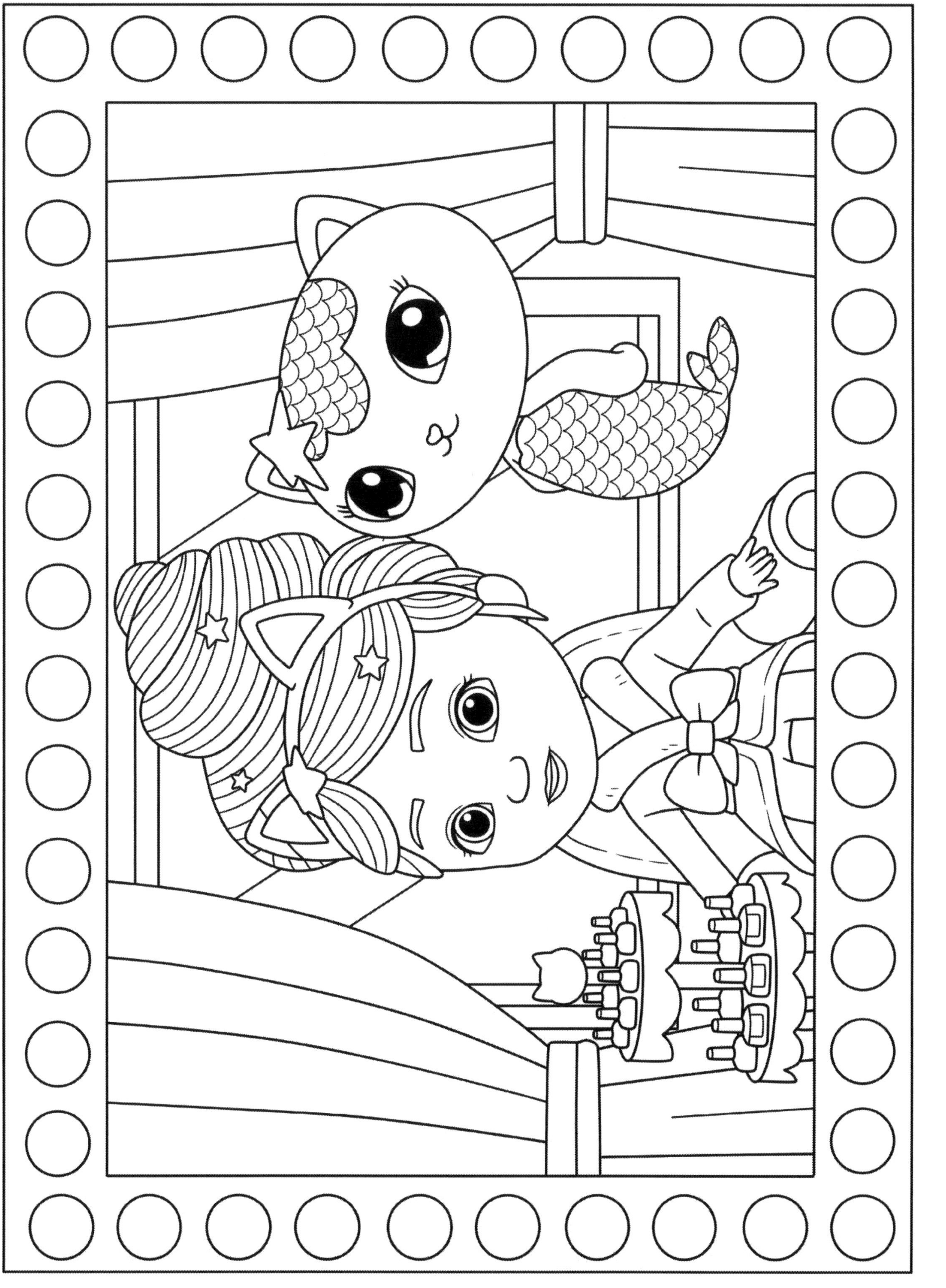

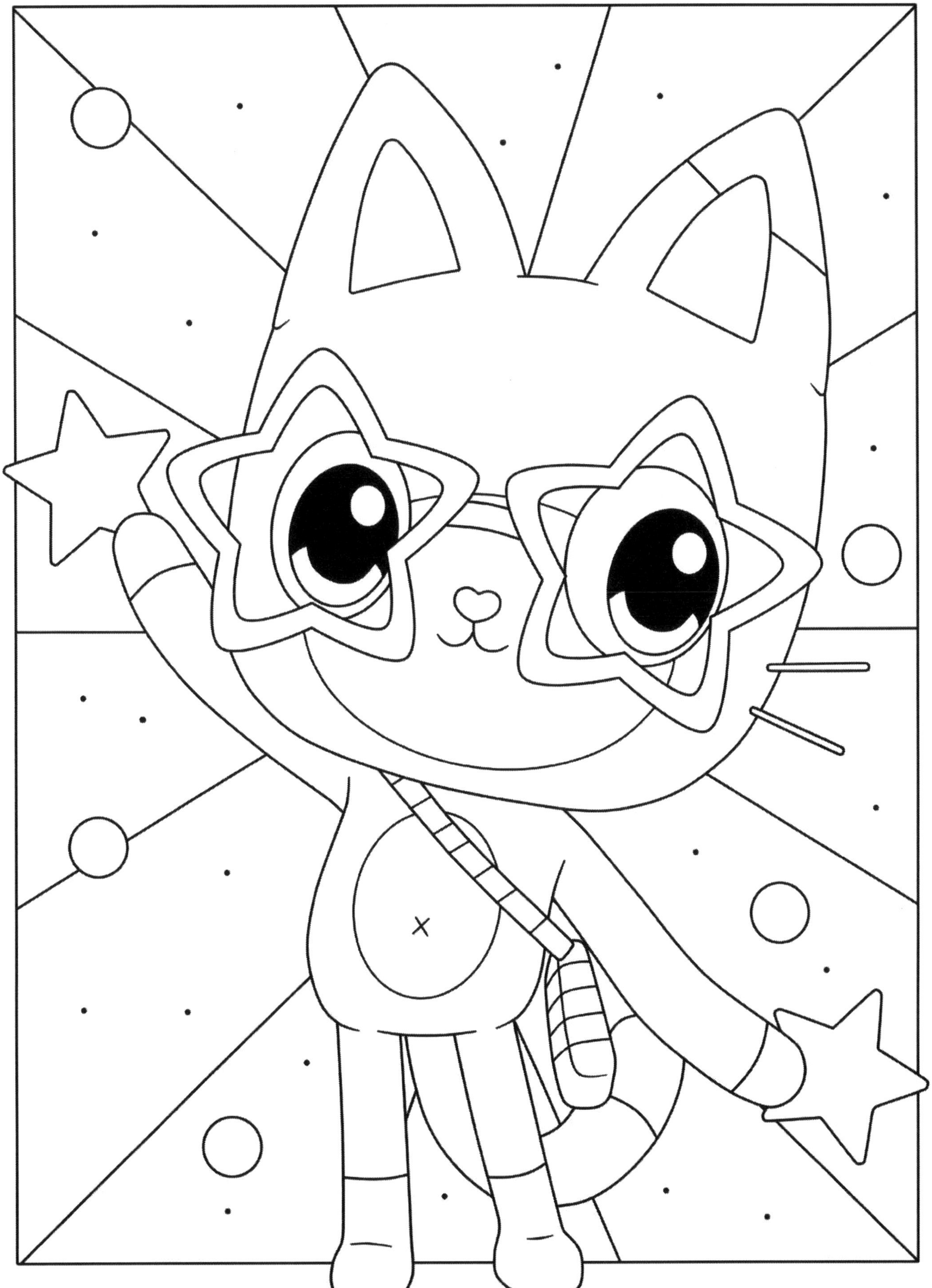

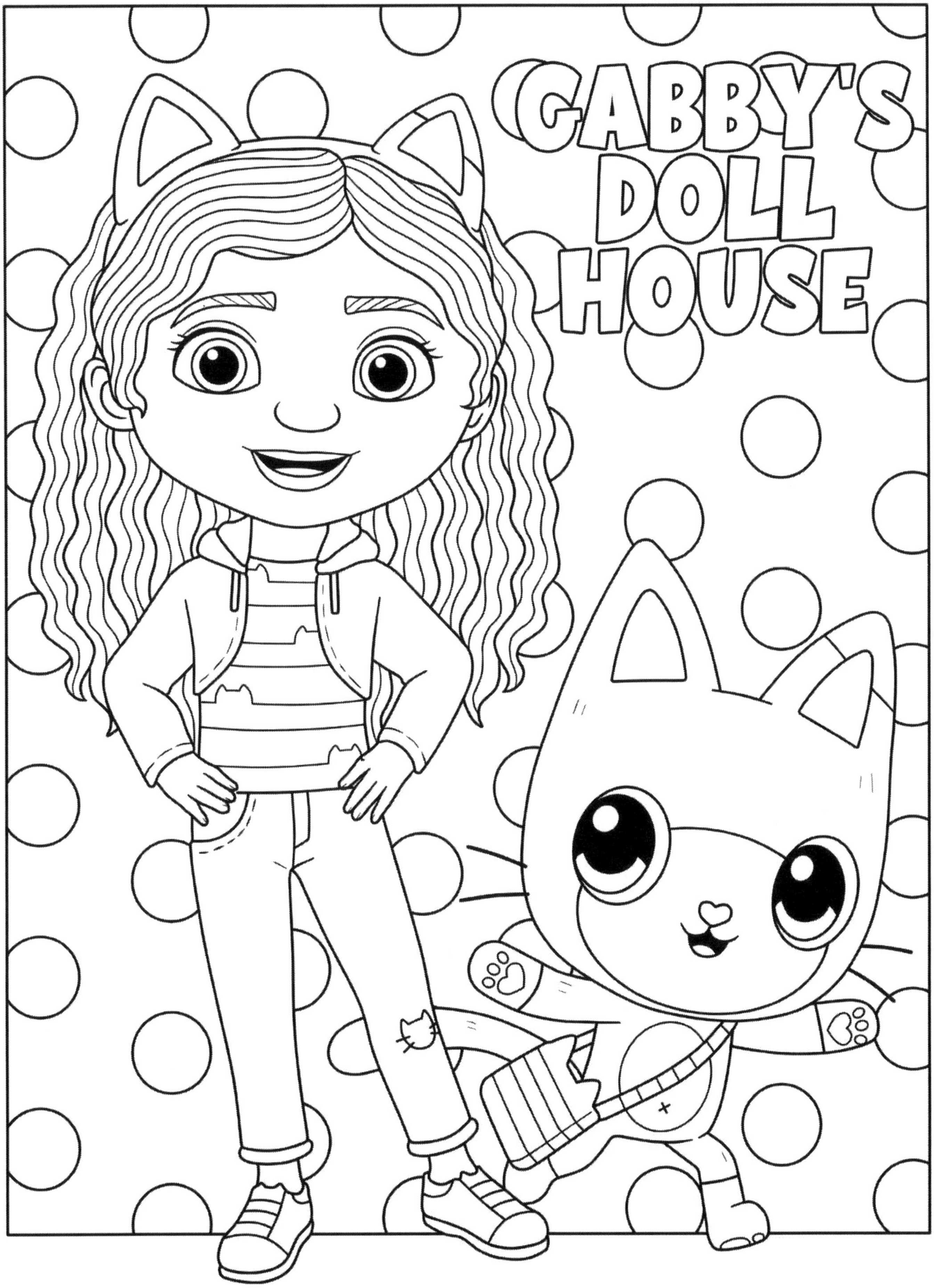
GABBY'S
DOLL
HOUSE

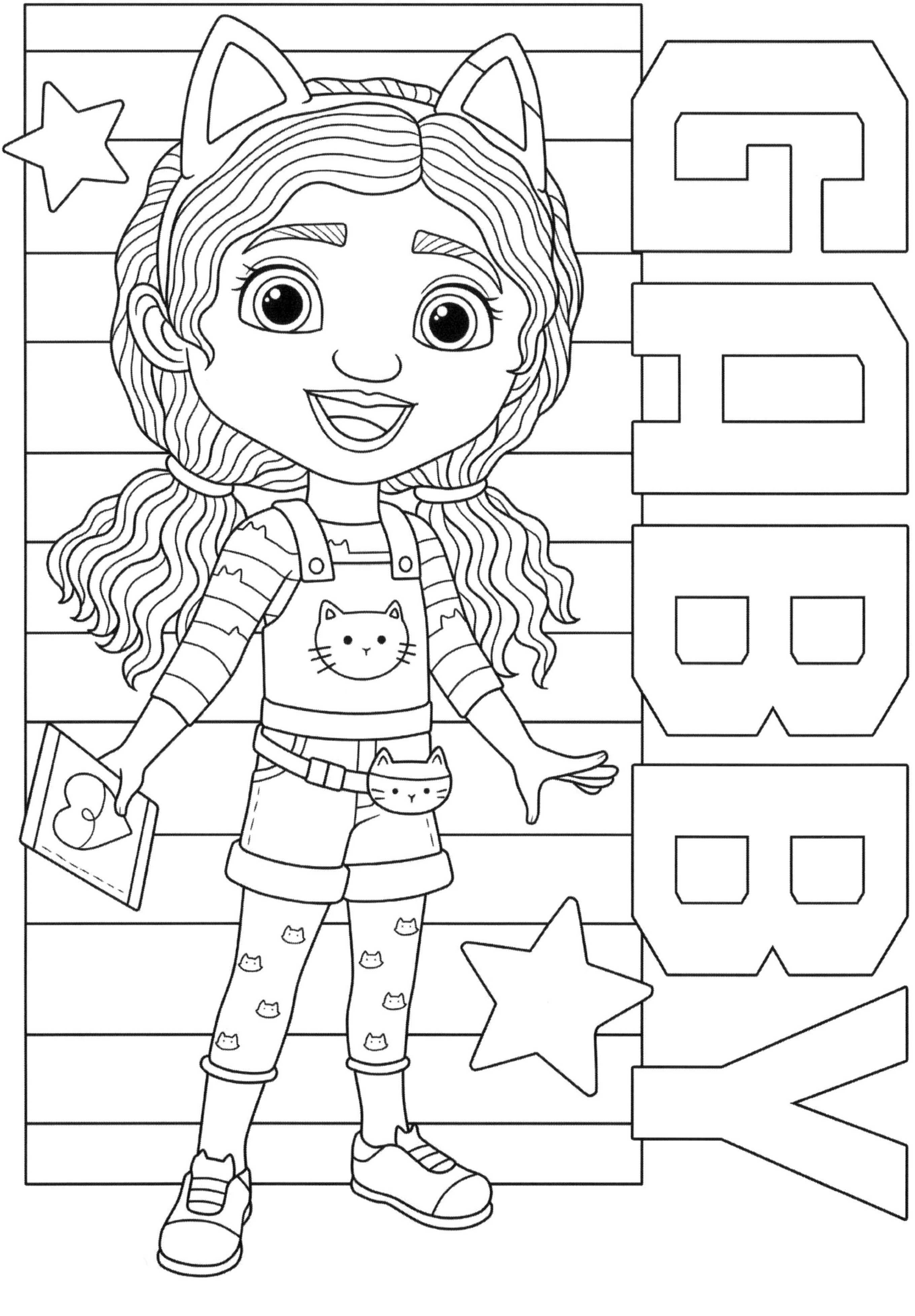
GABBY

PANDY PAWS

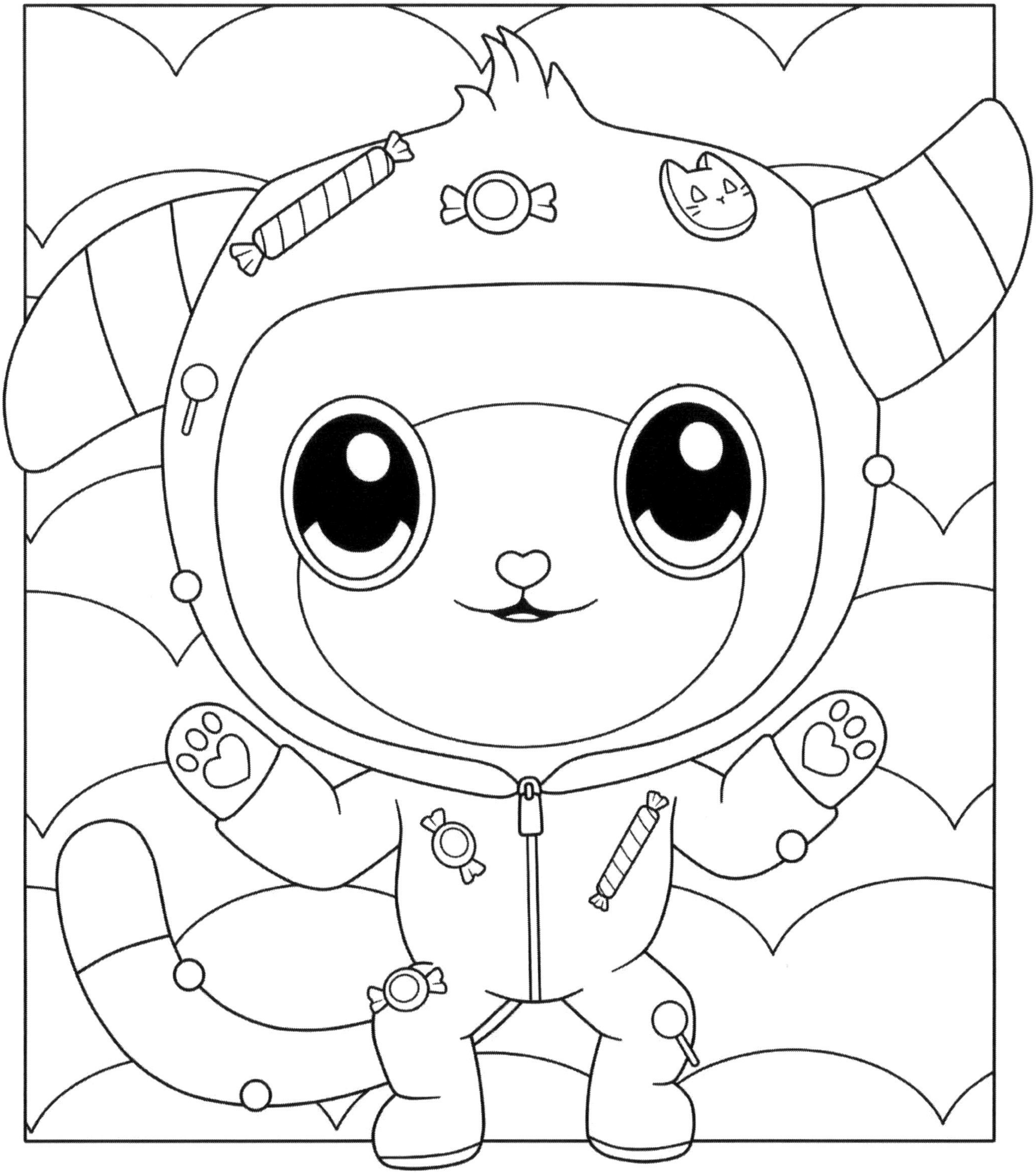

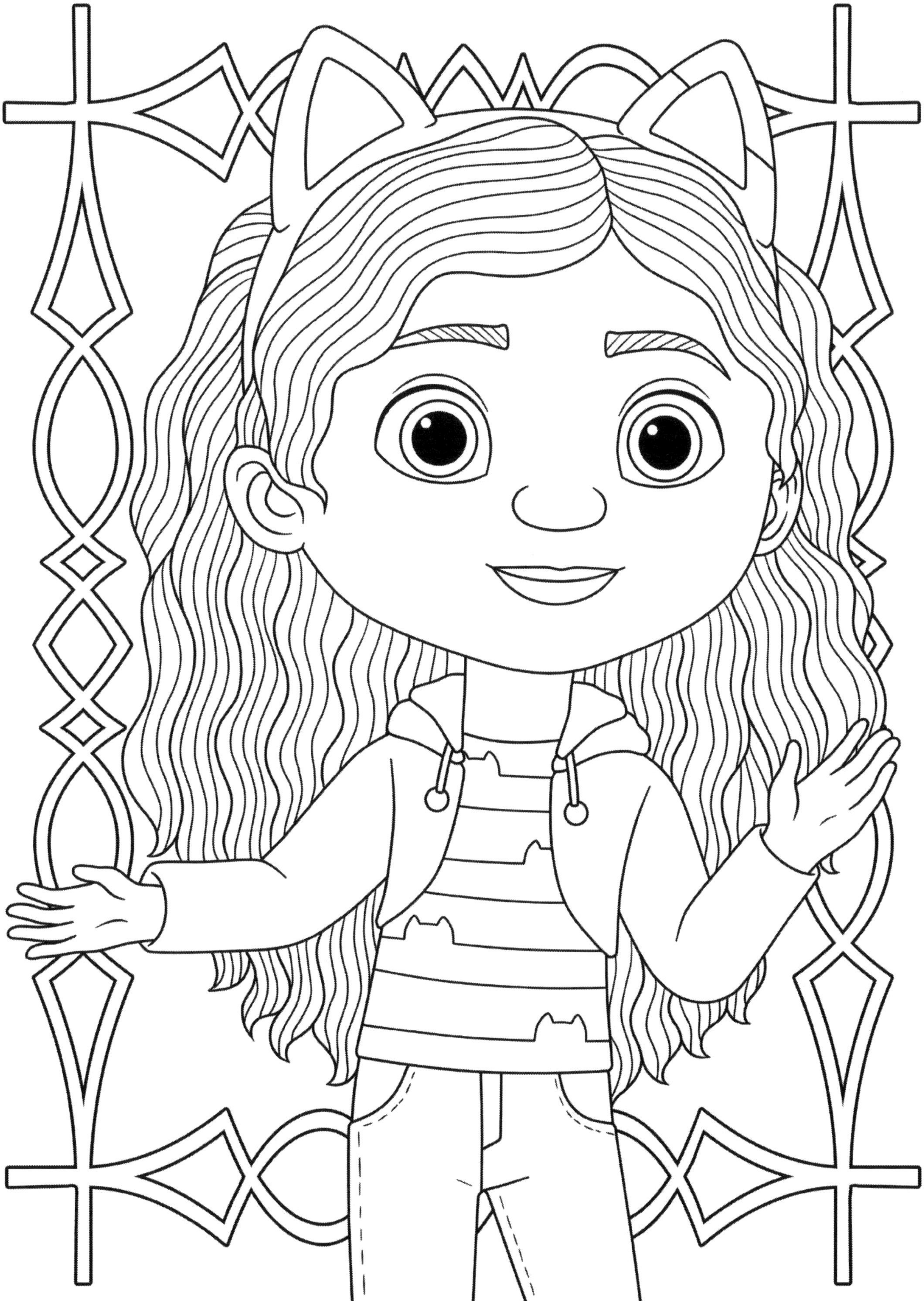

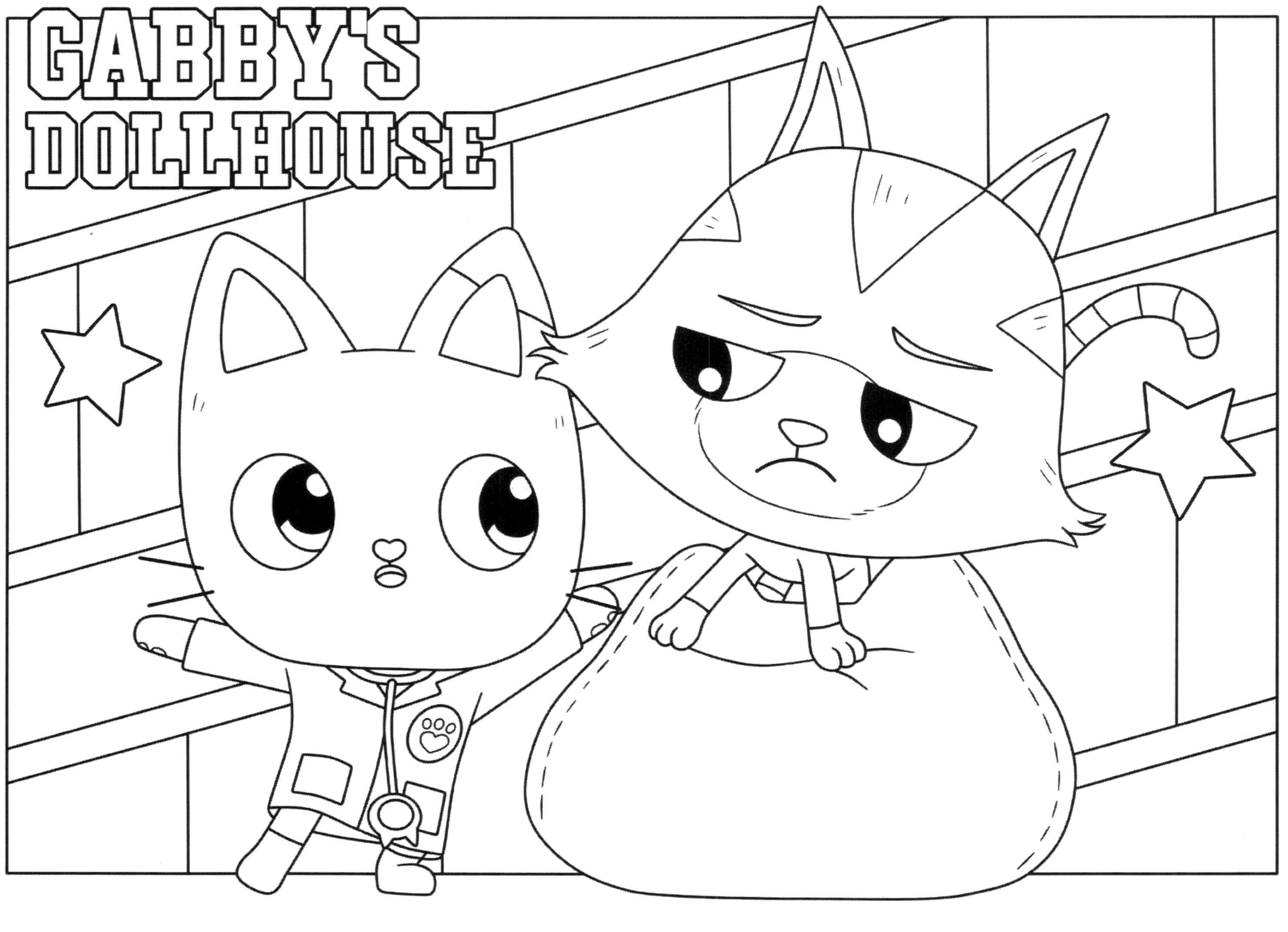
GABBY'S
DOLLHOUSE

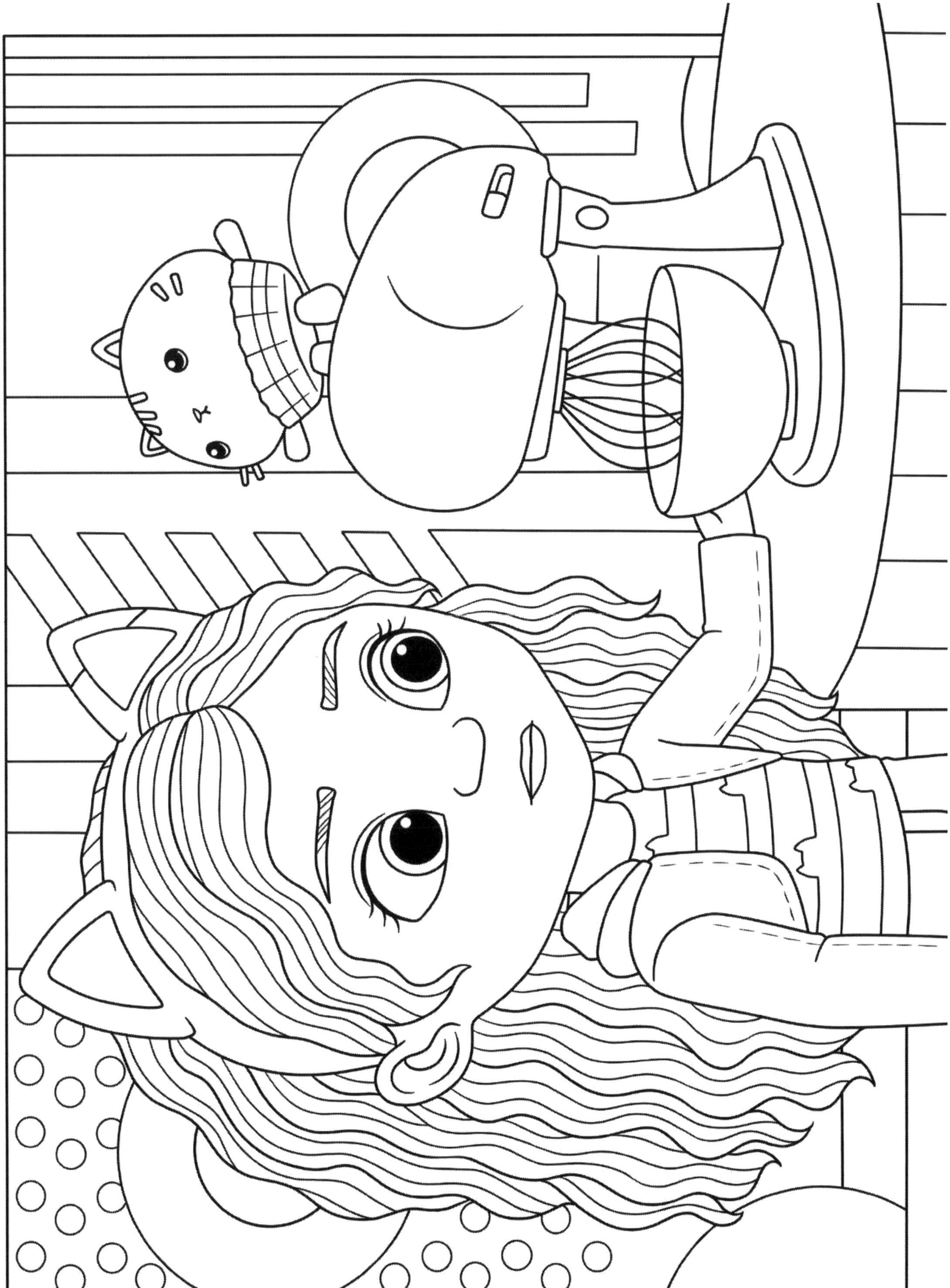

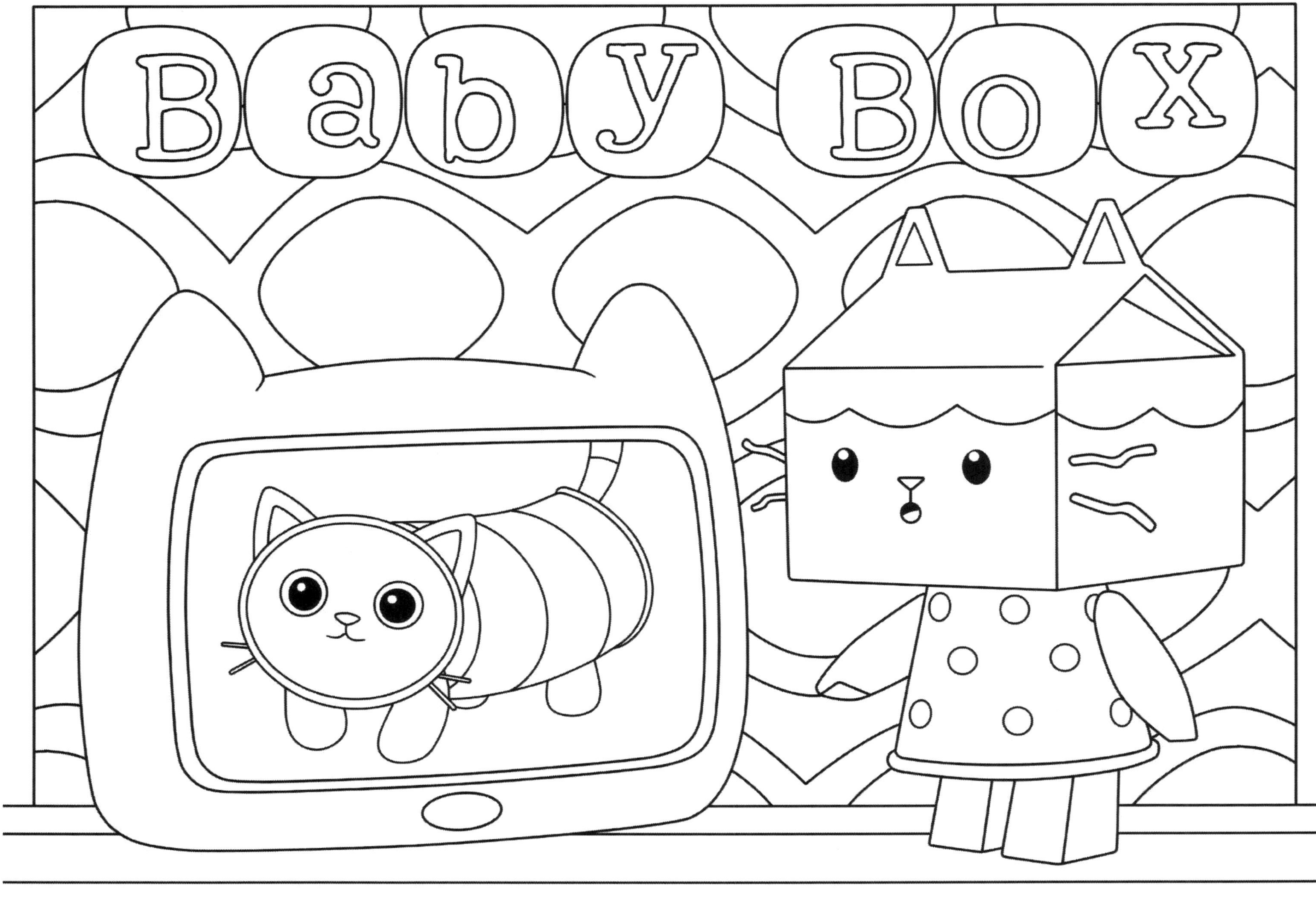
Baby Box

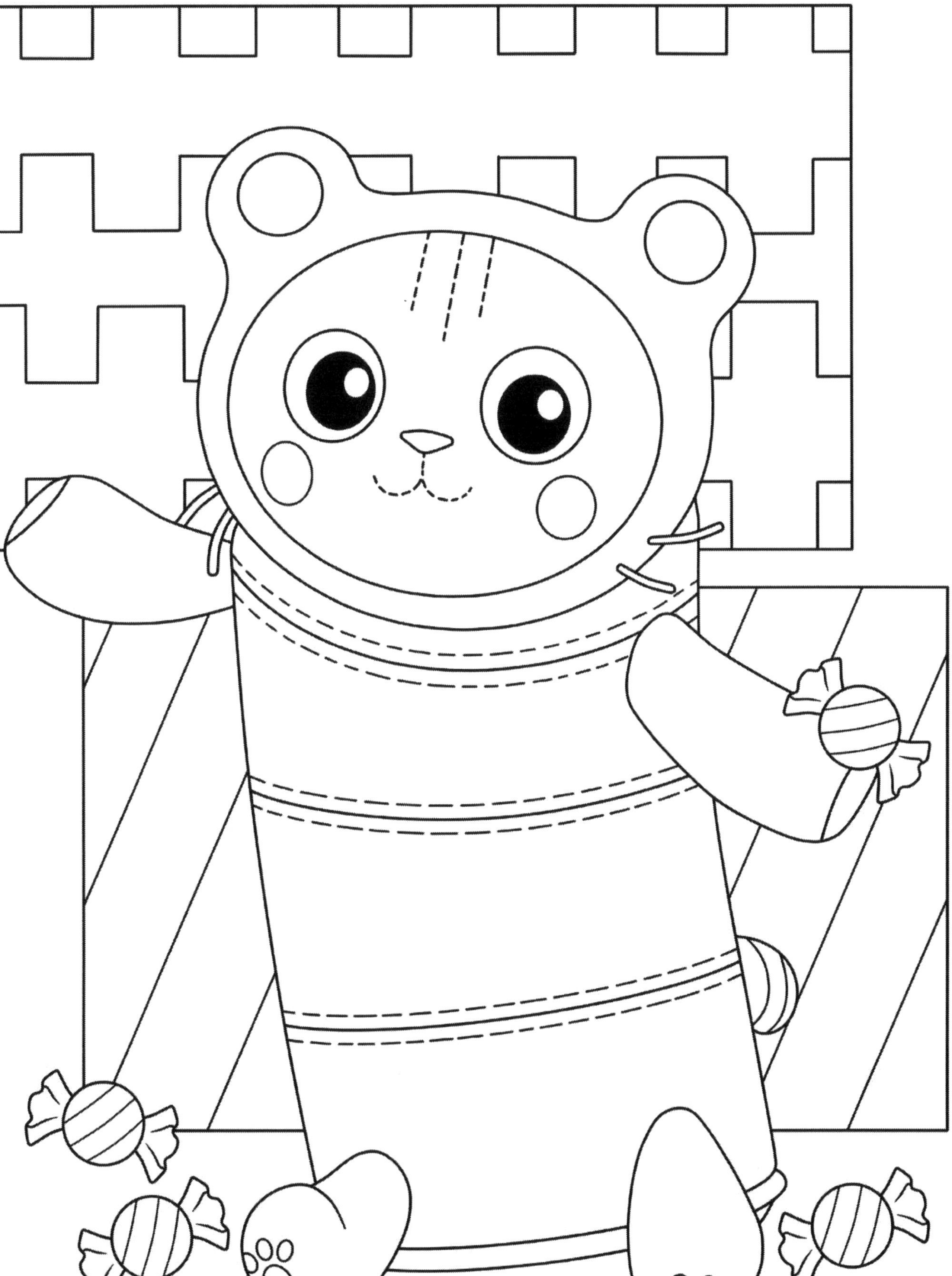

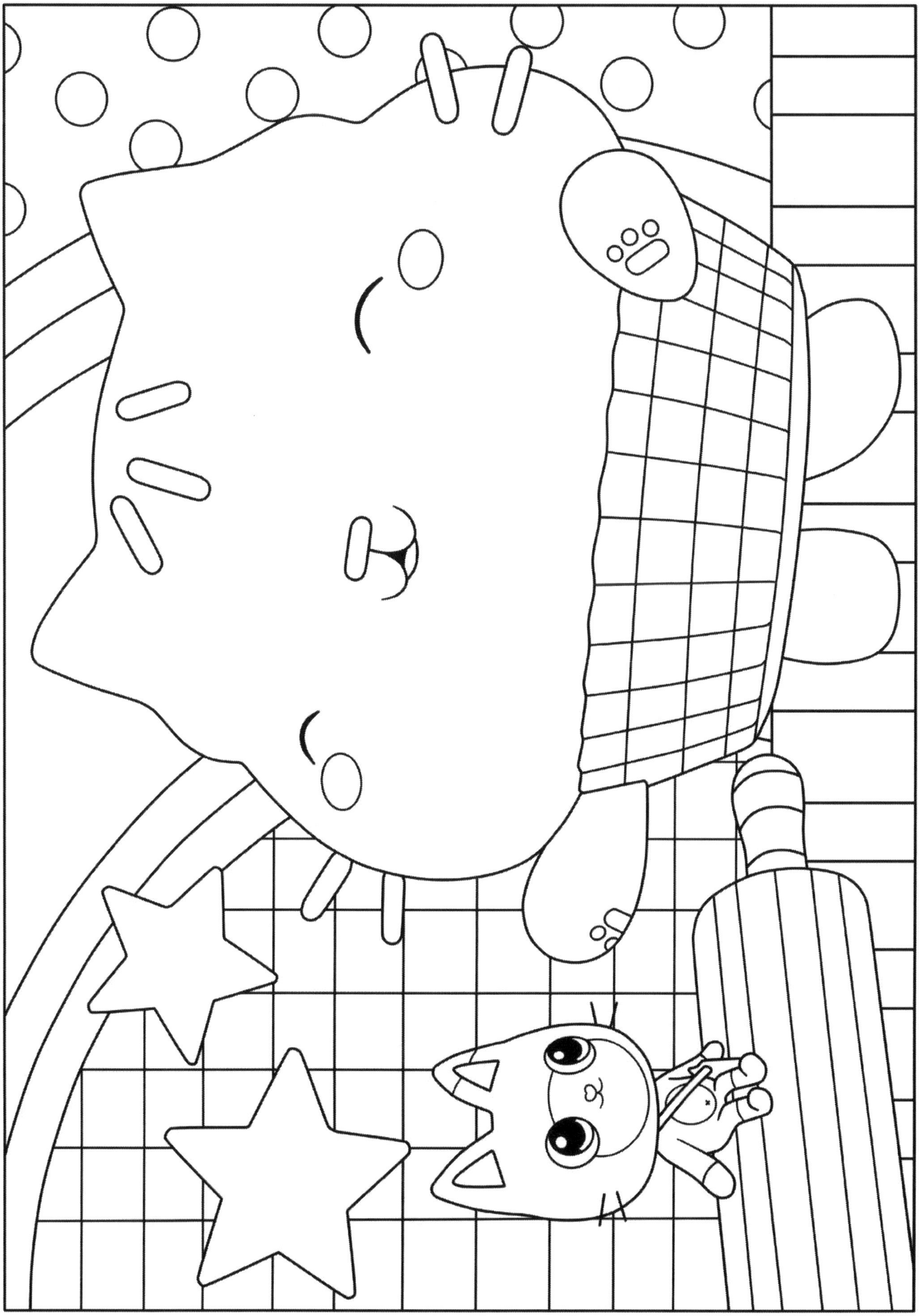

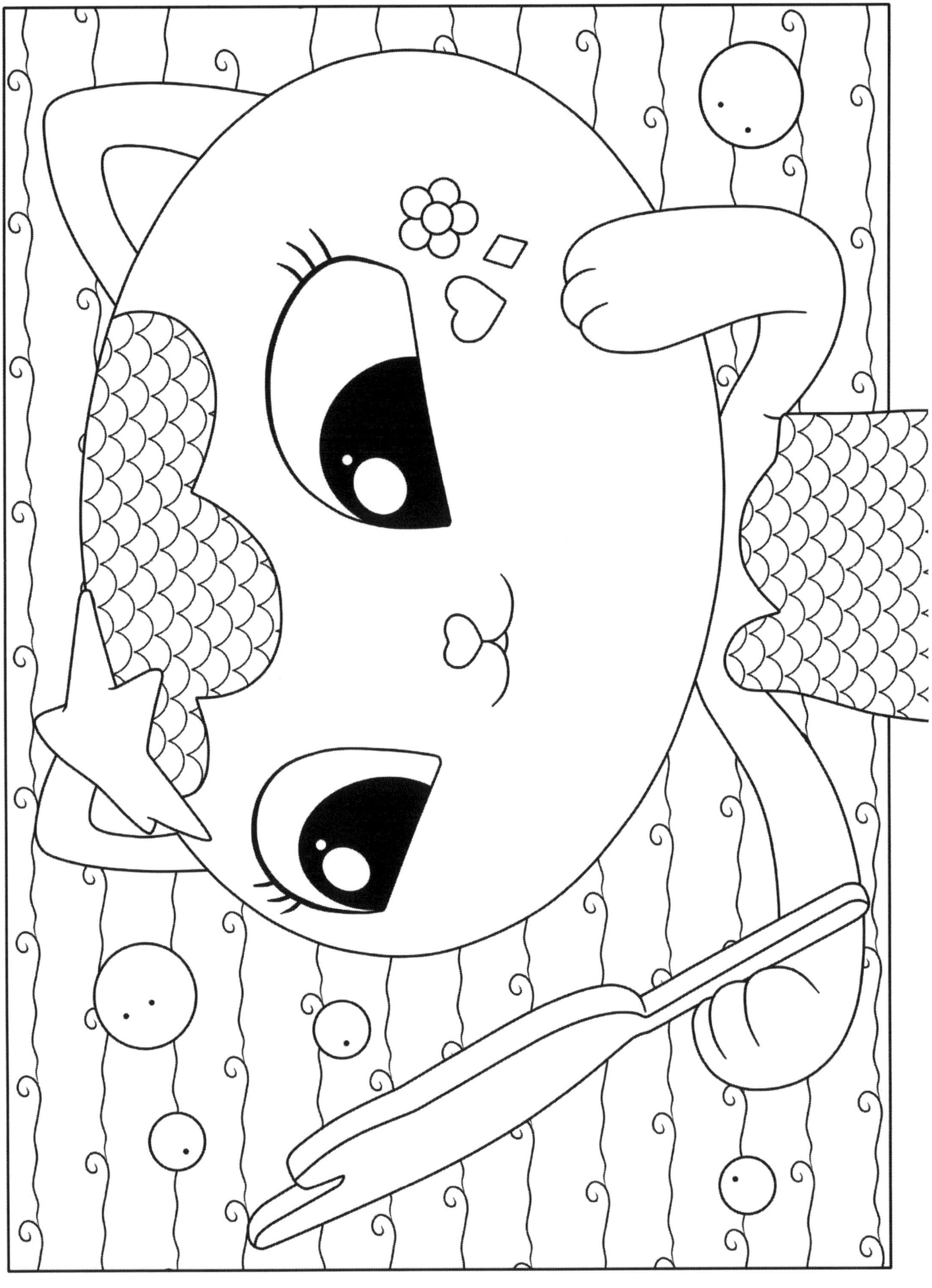

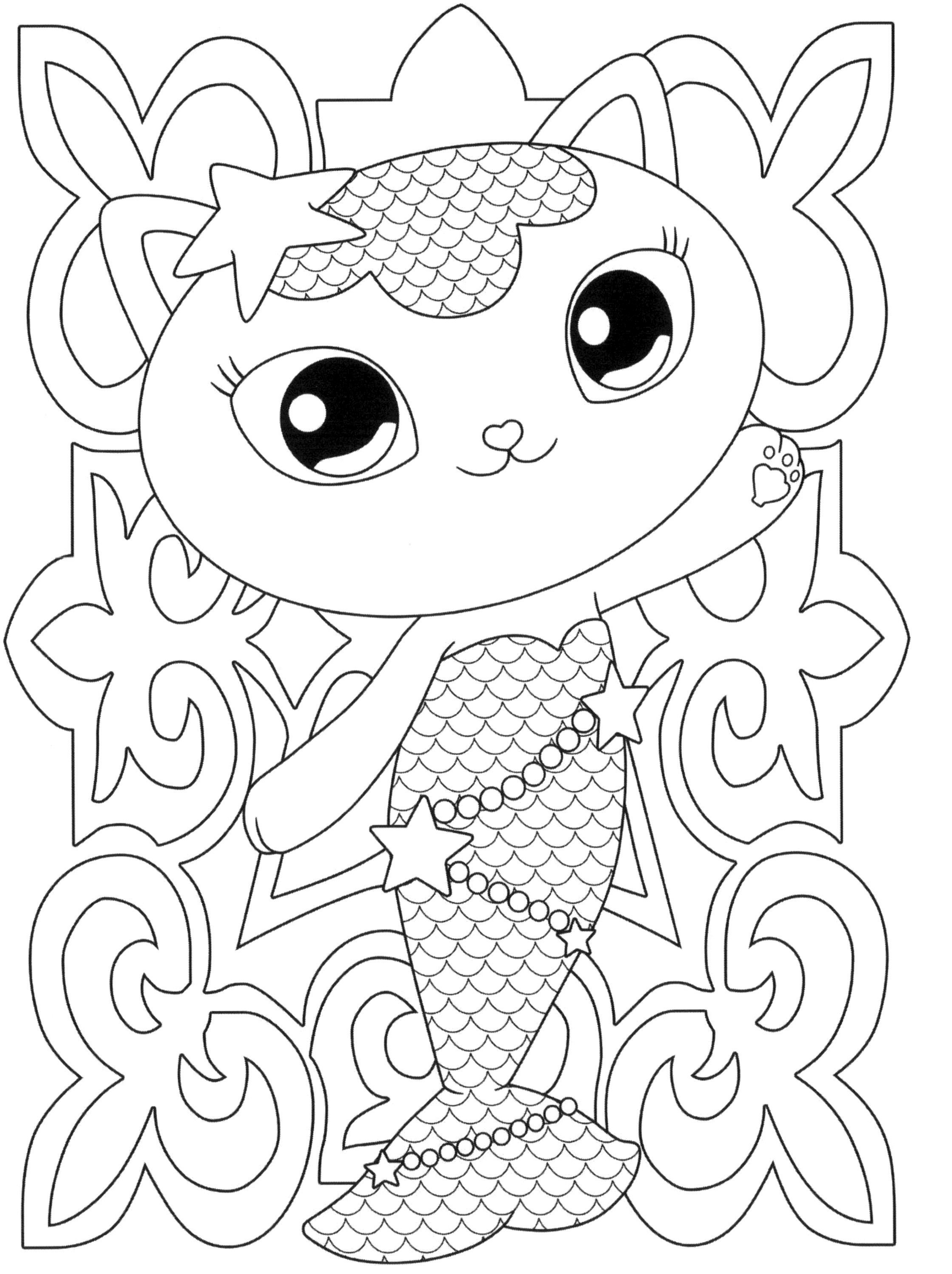

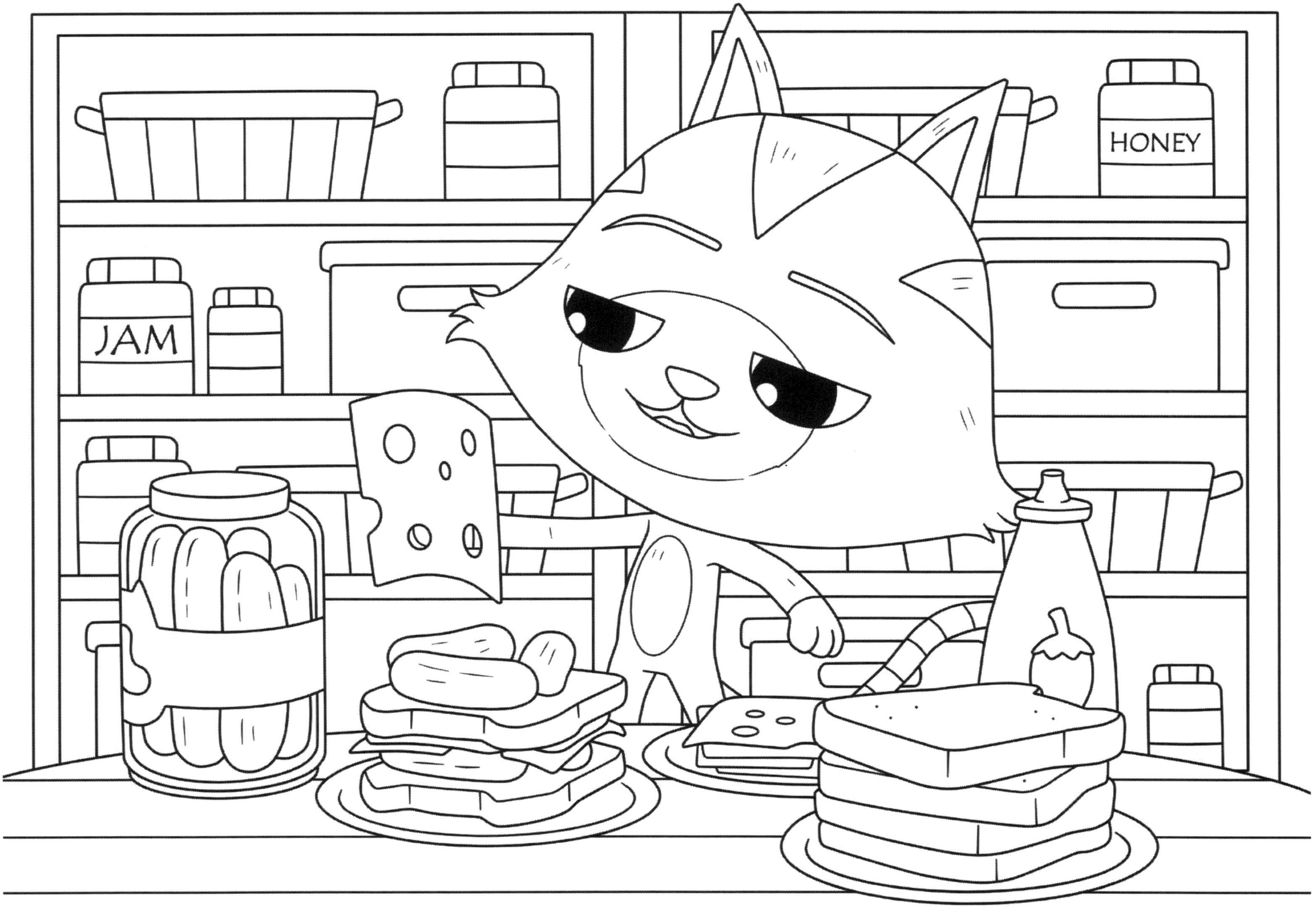
HONEY
JAM

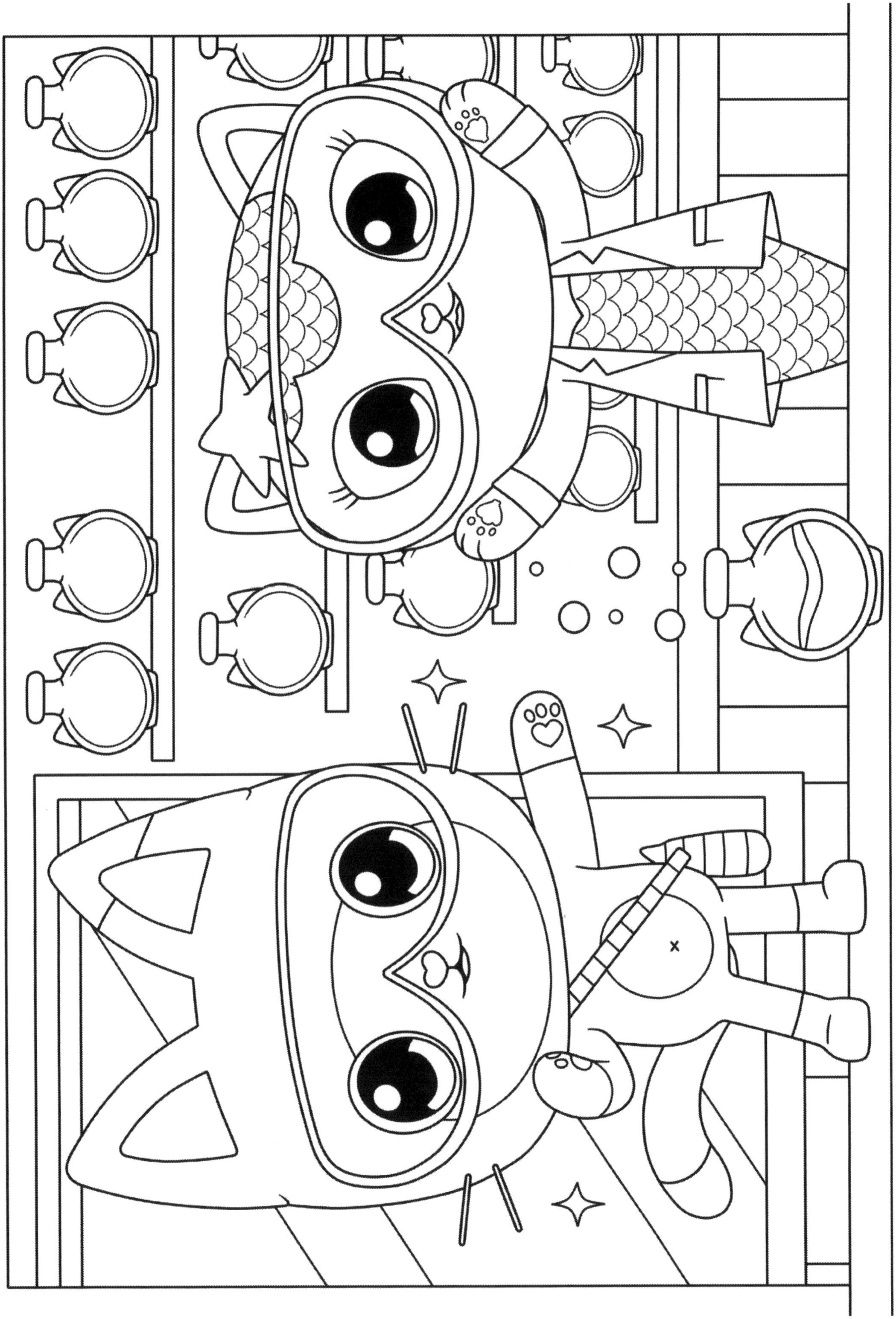

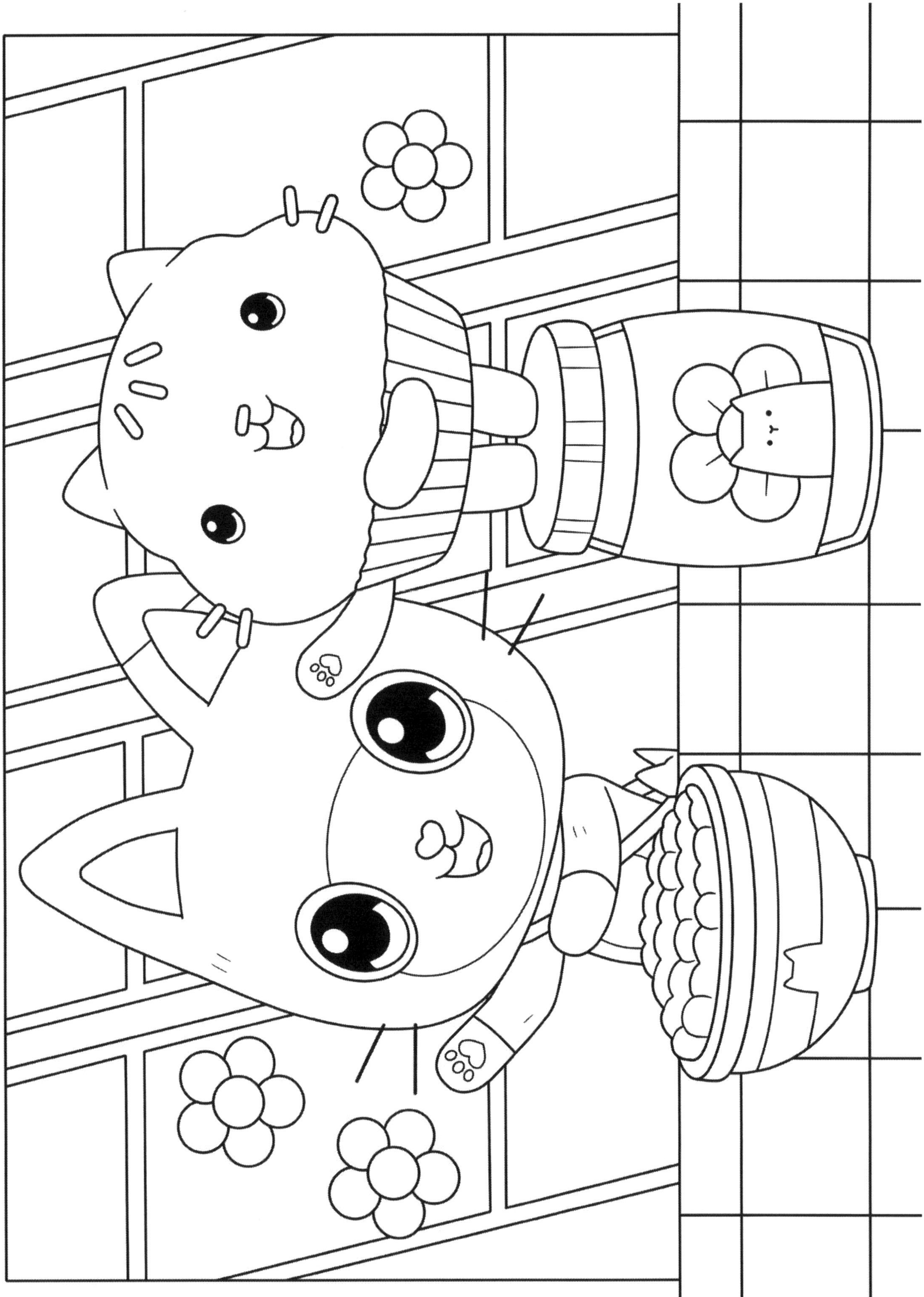

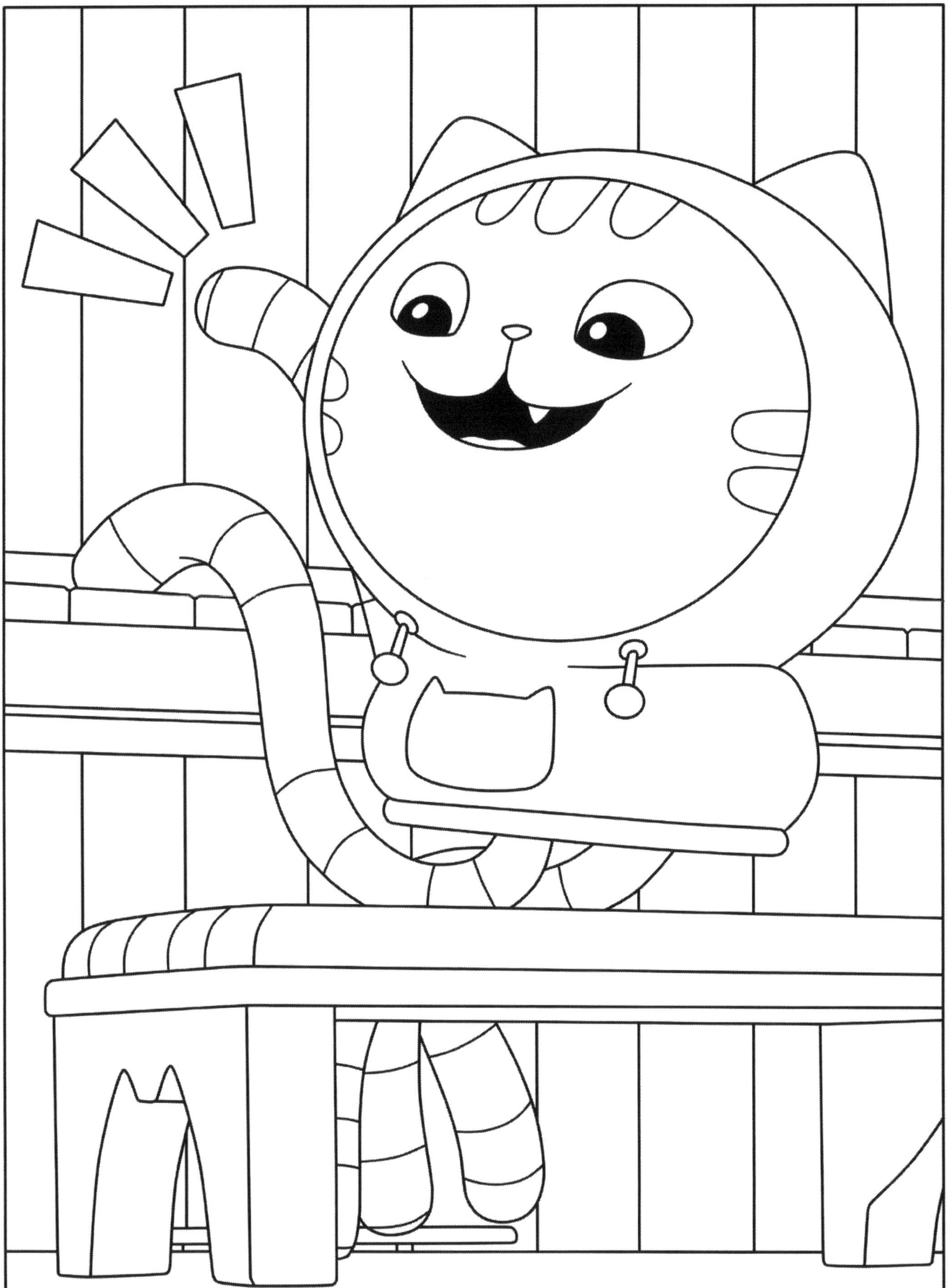

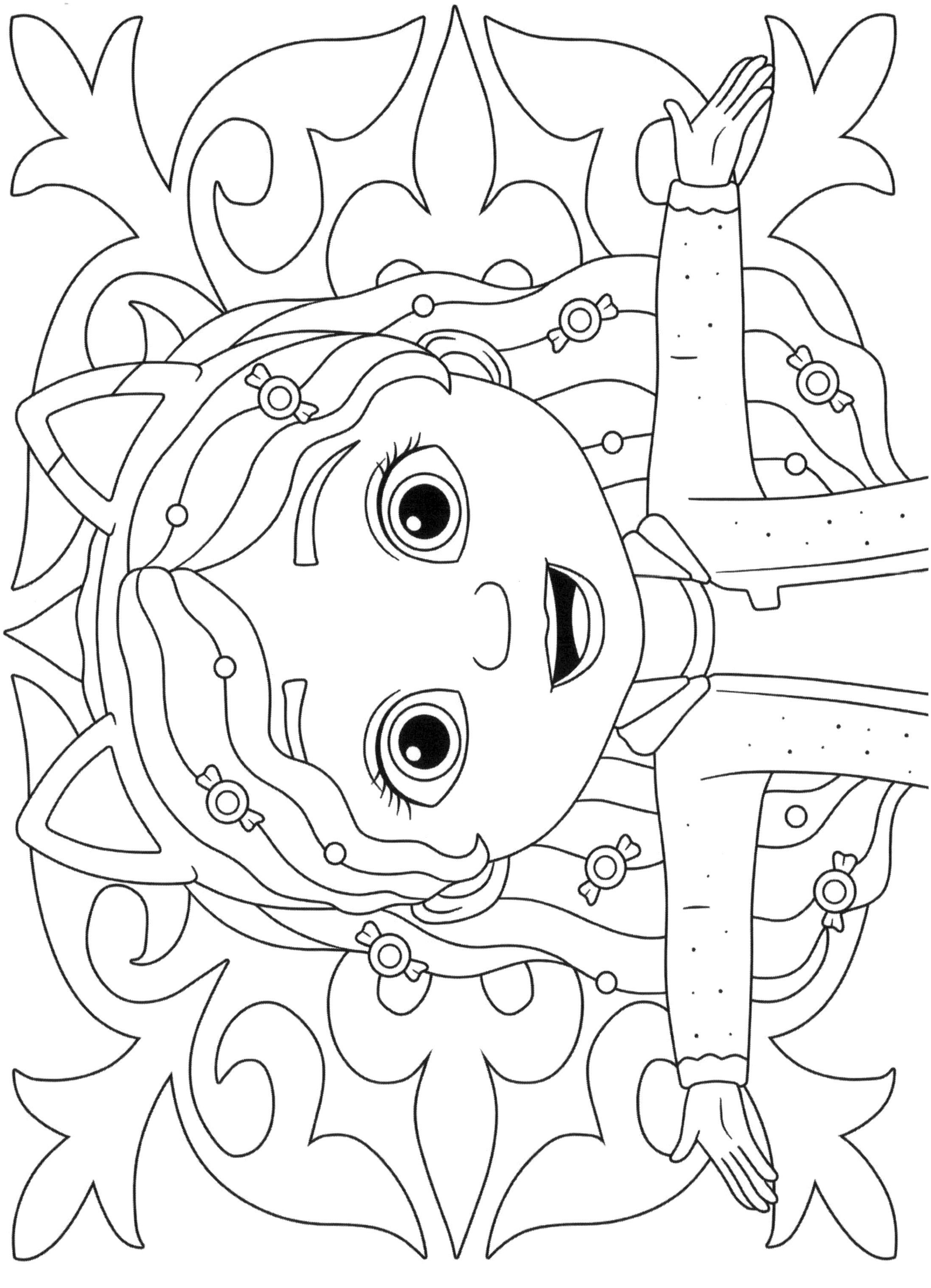

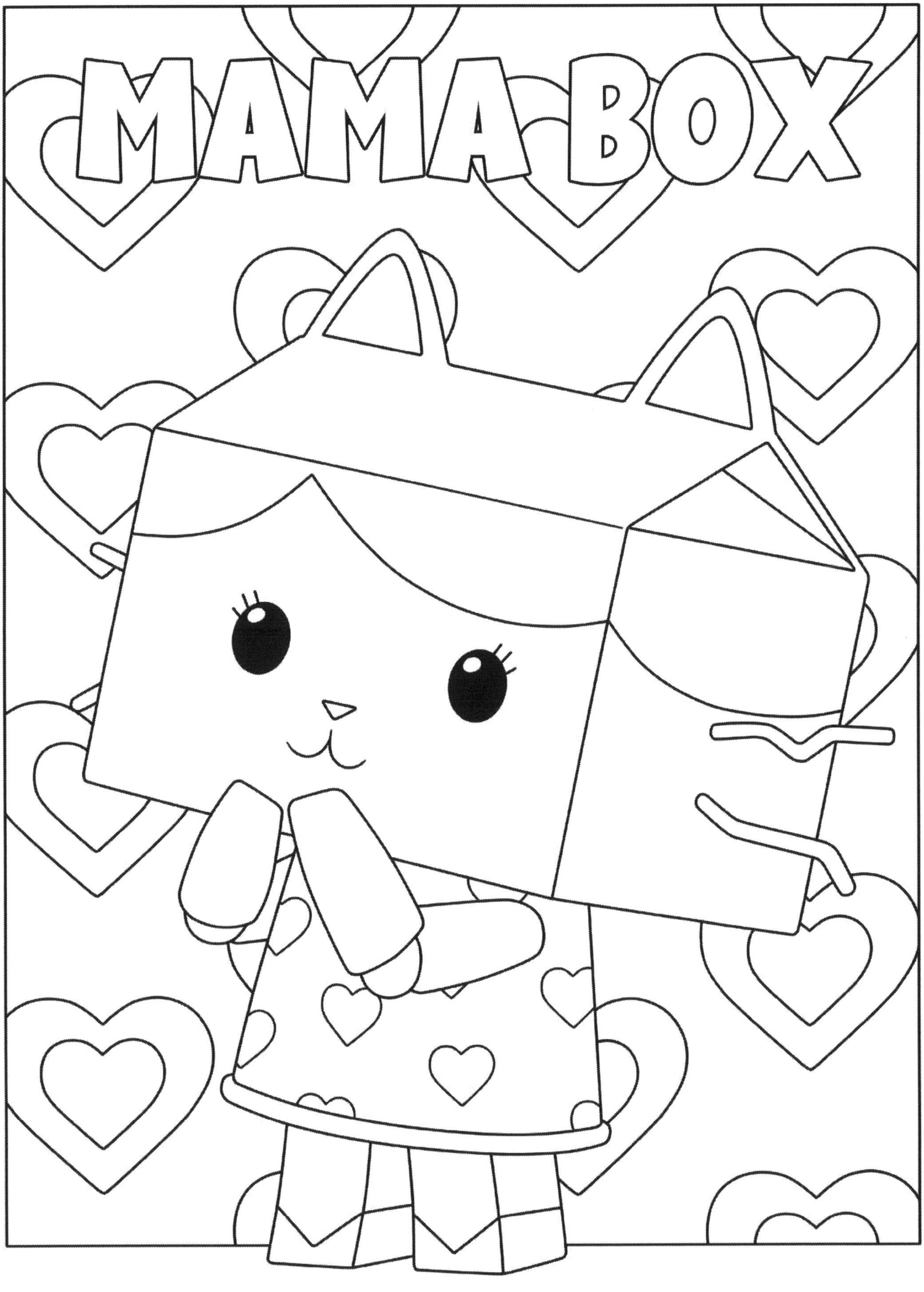
MAMA BOX

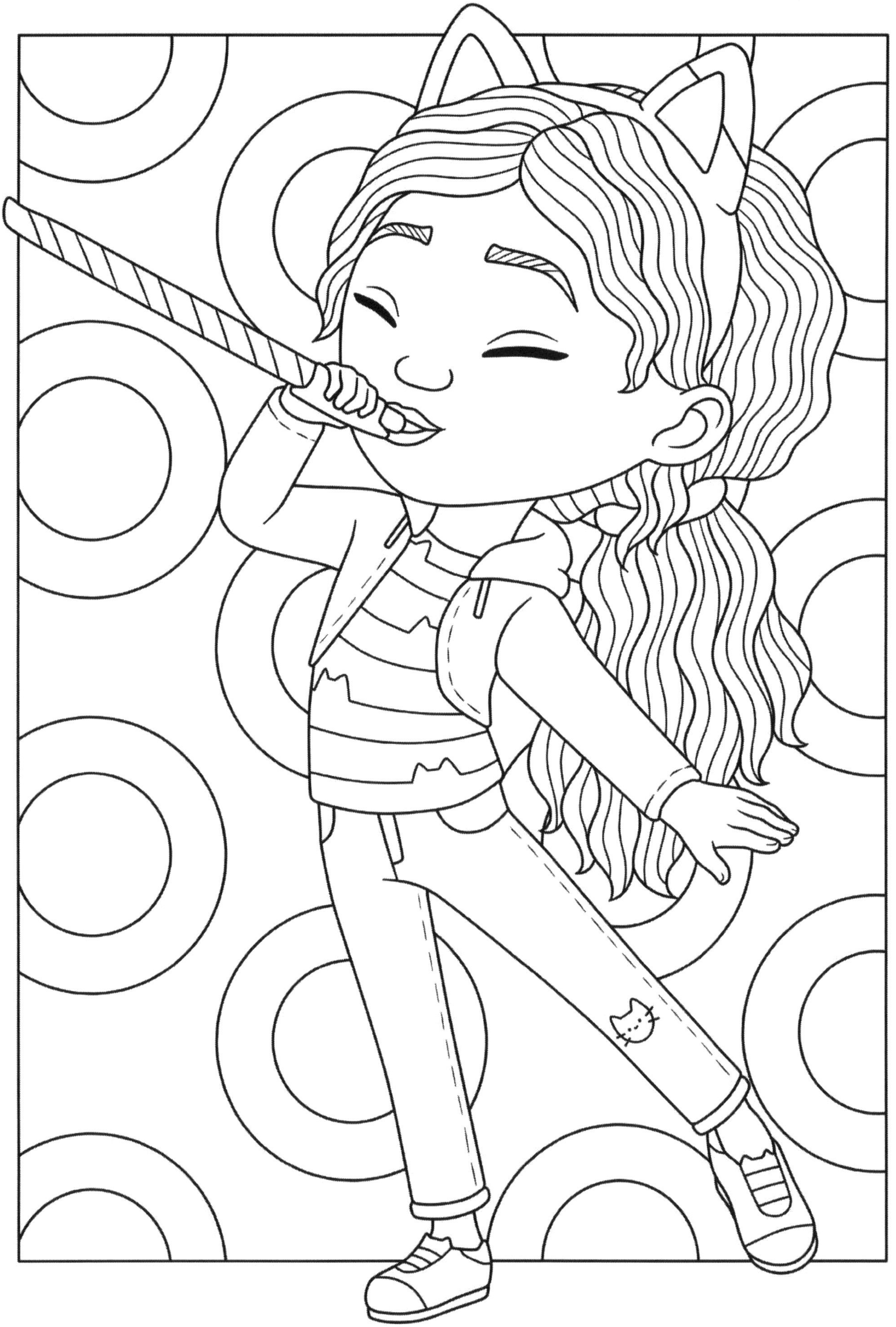

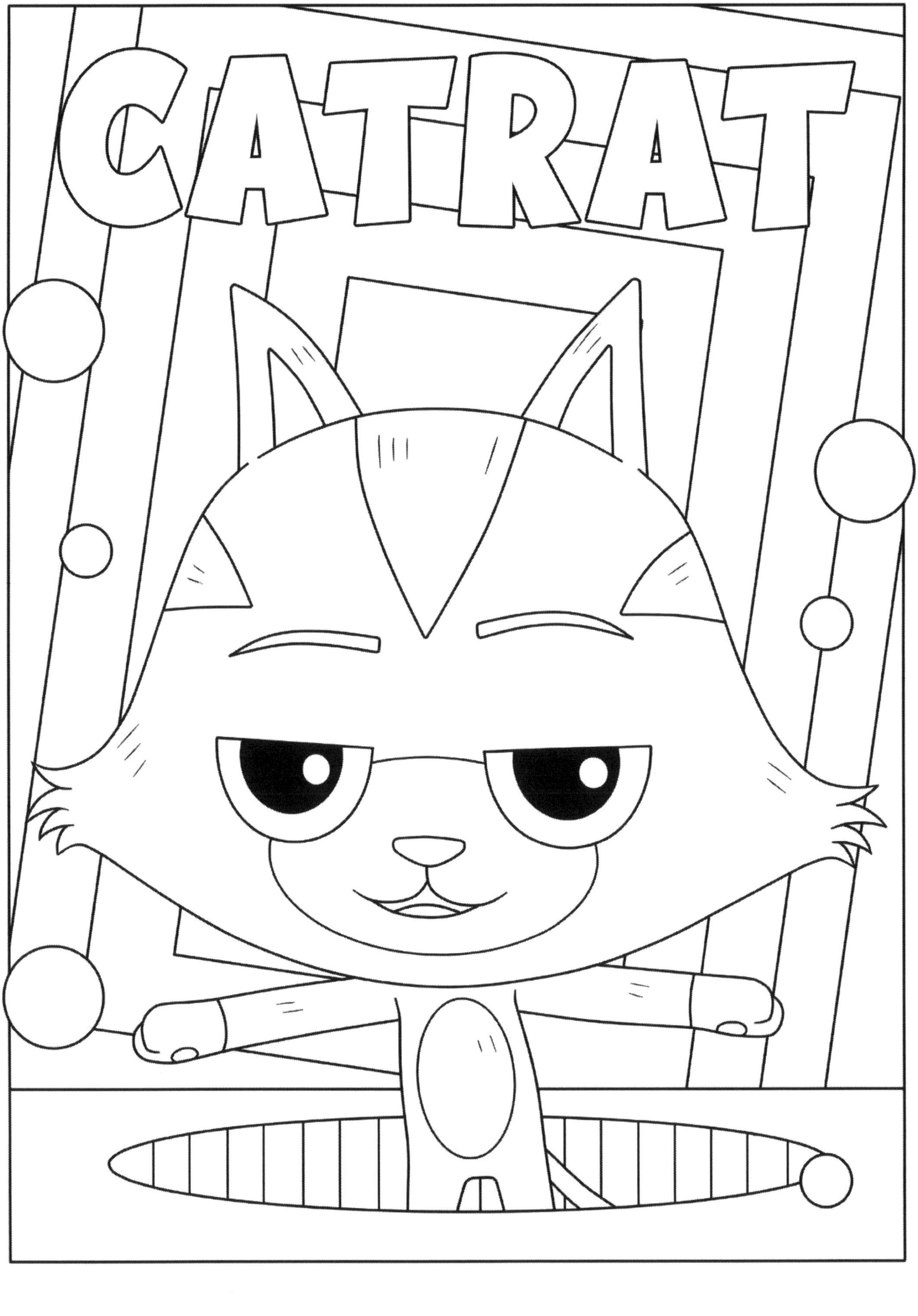
CATRAT

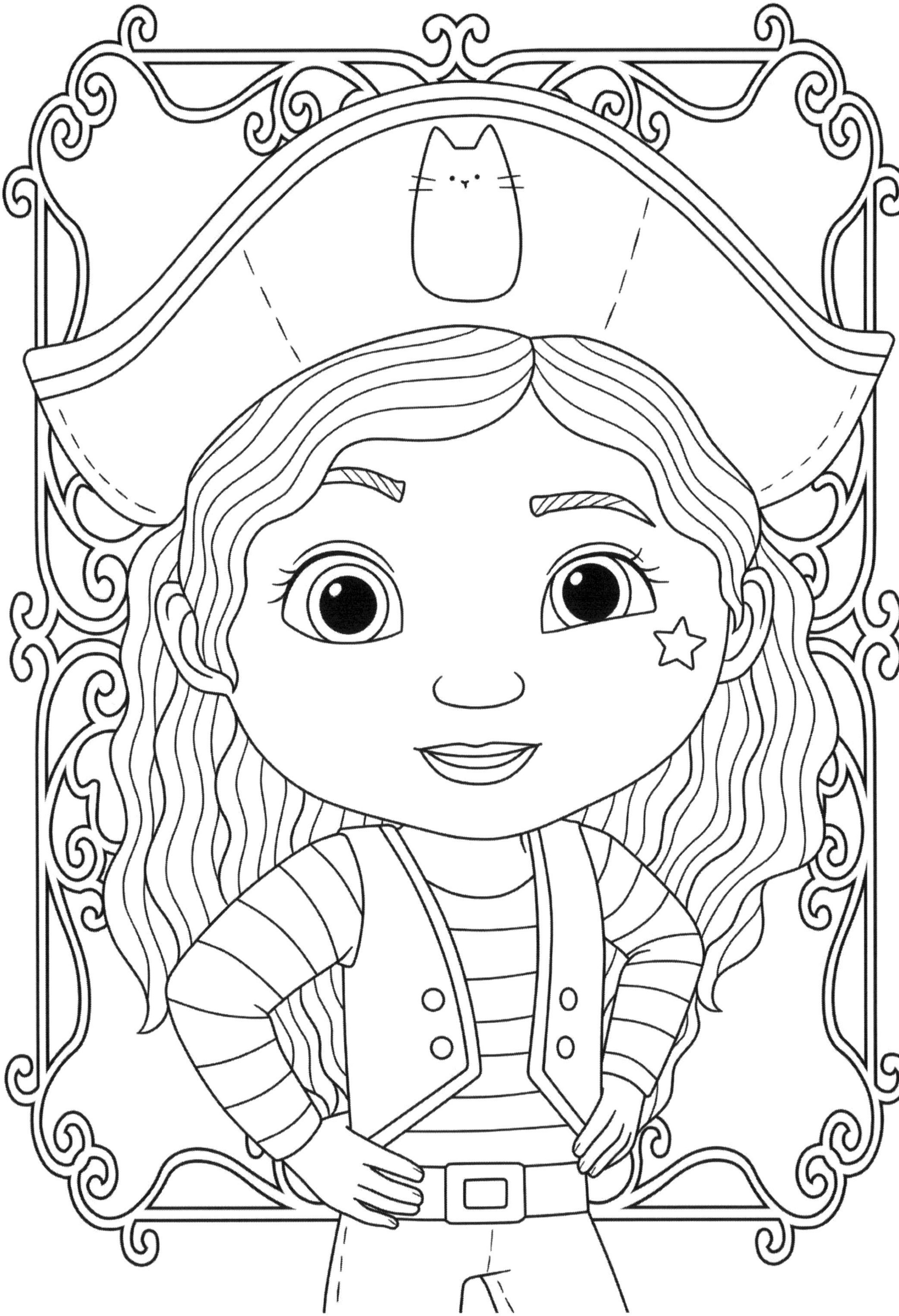

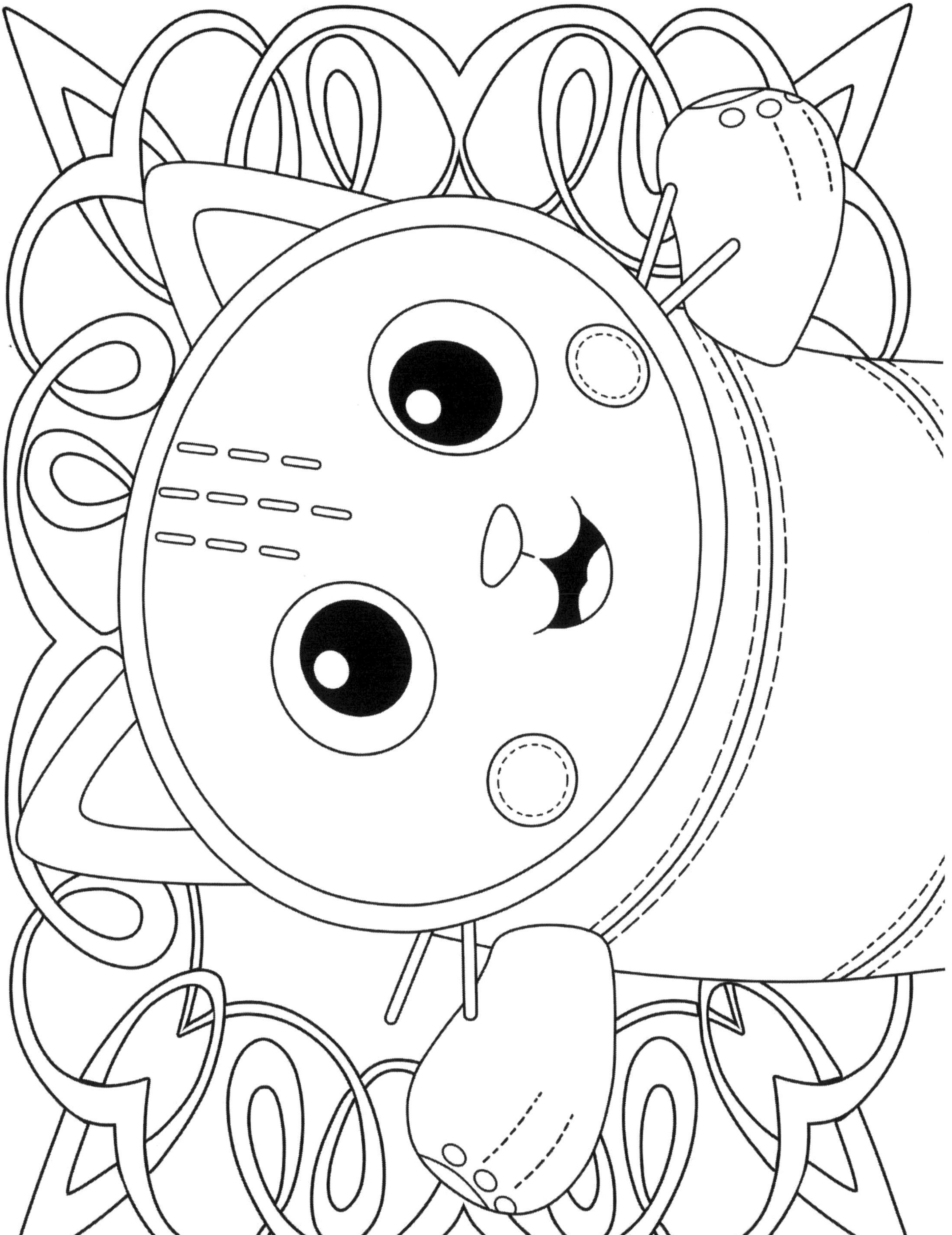

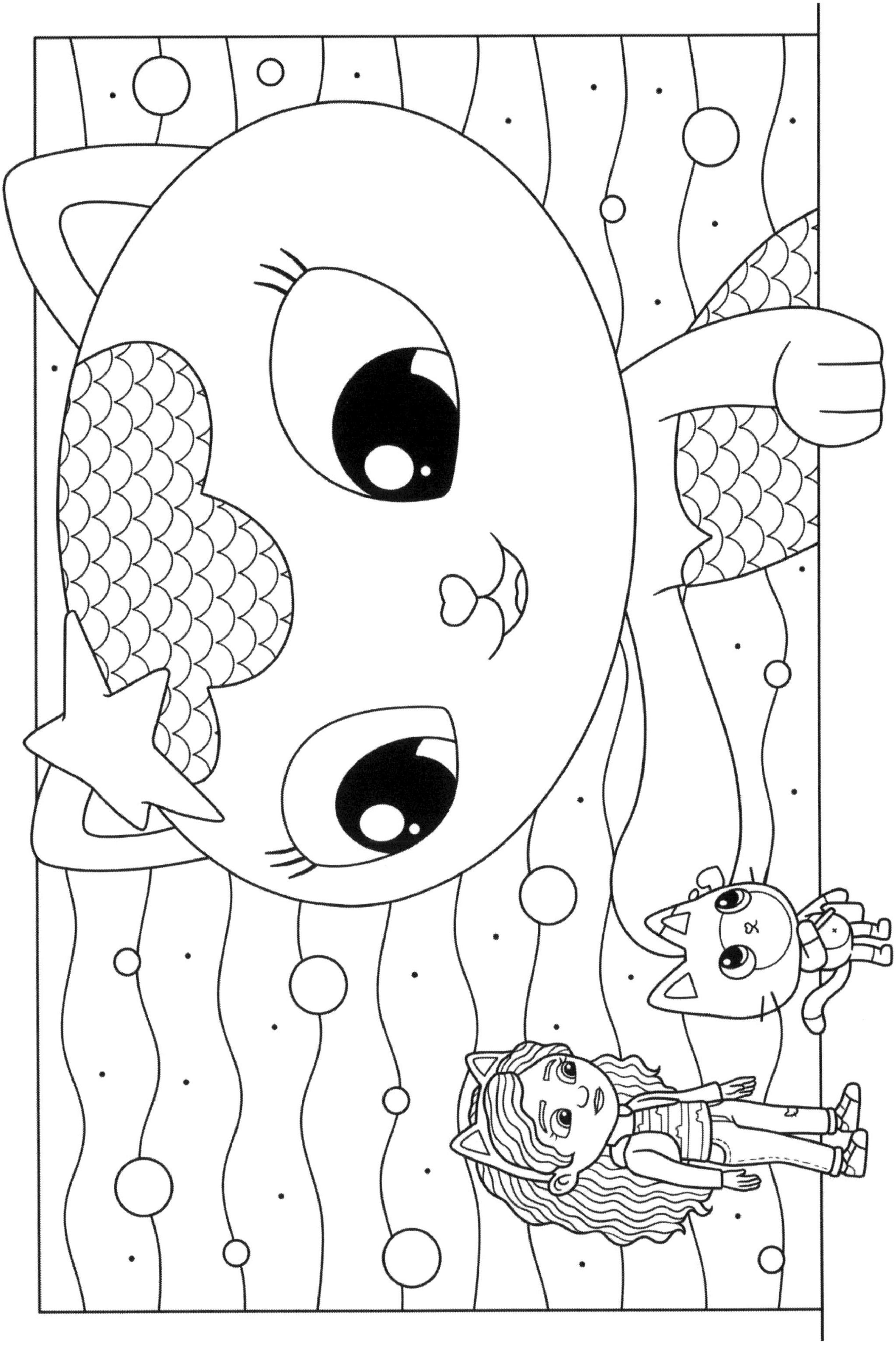

PLAYTIME!

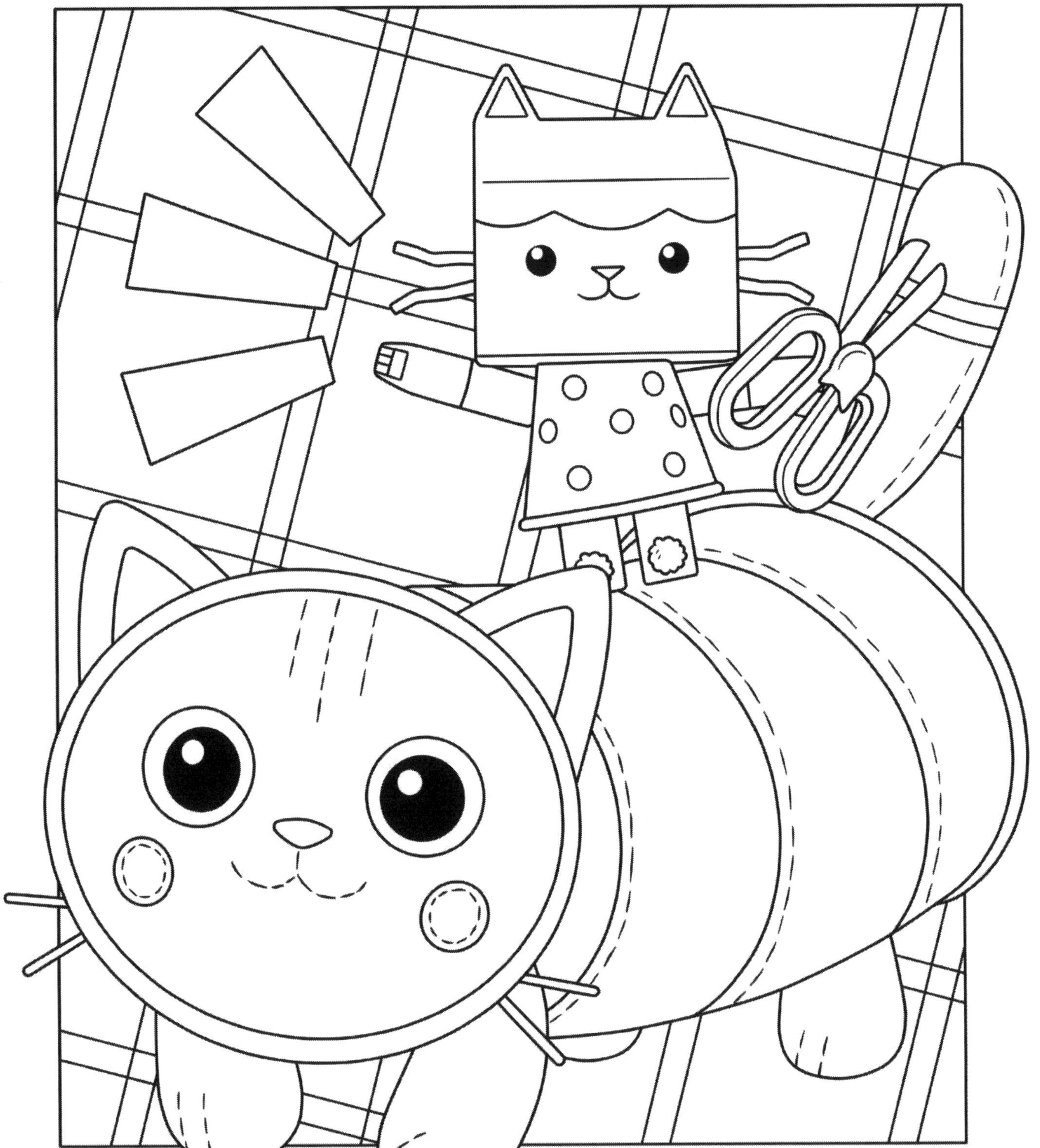

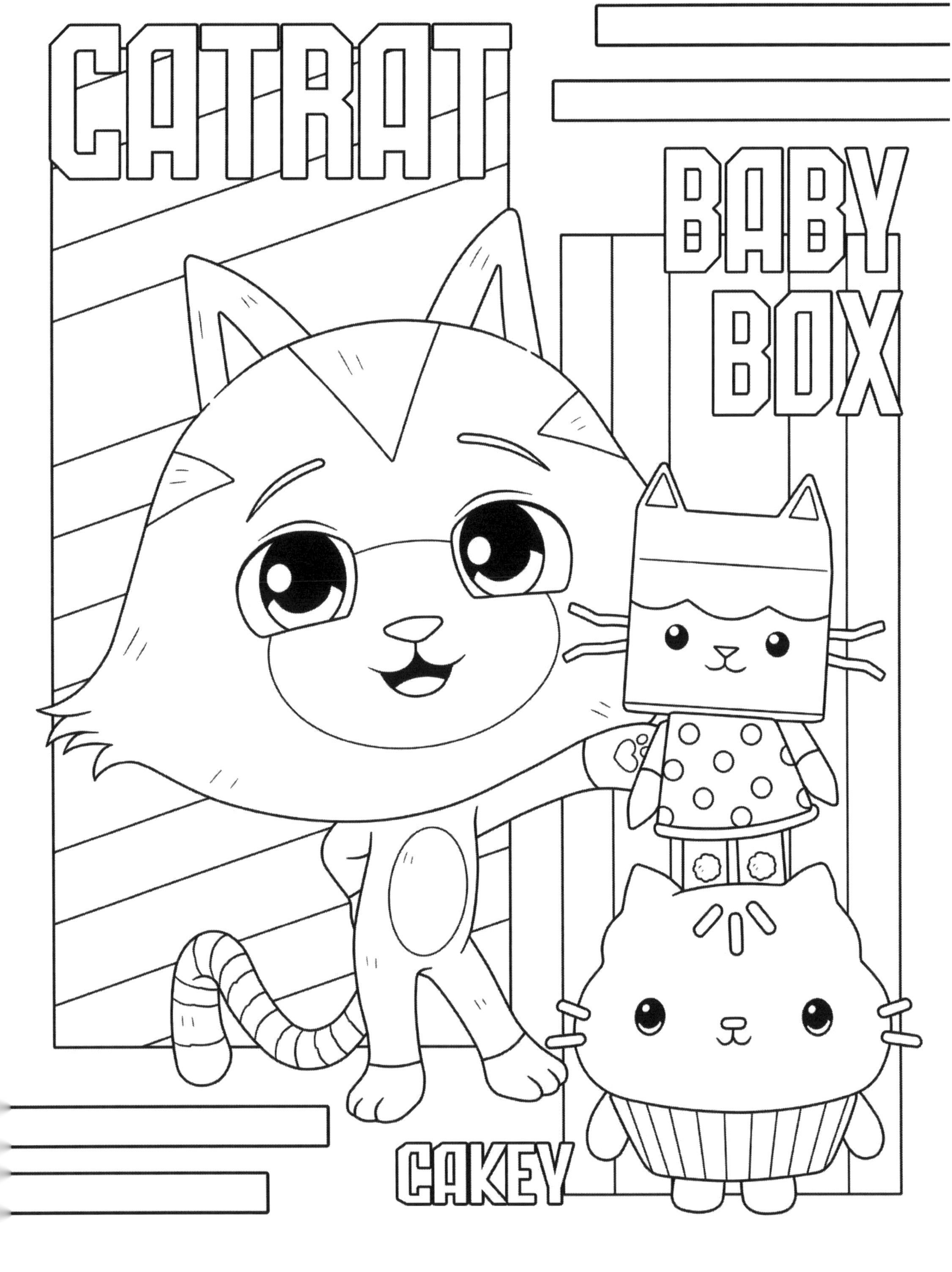
CATRAT
BABY BOX
CAKEY

PANDY Paws

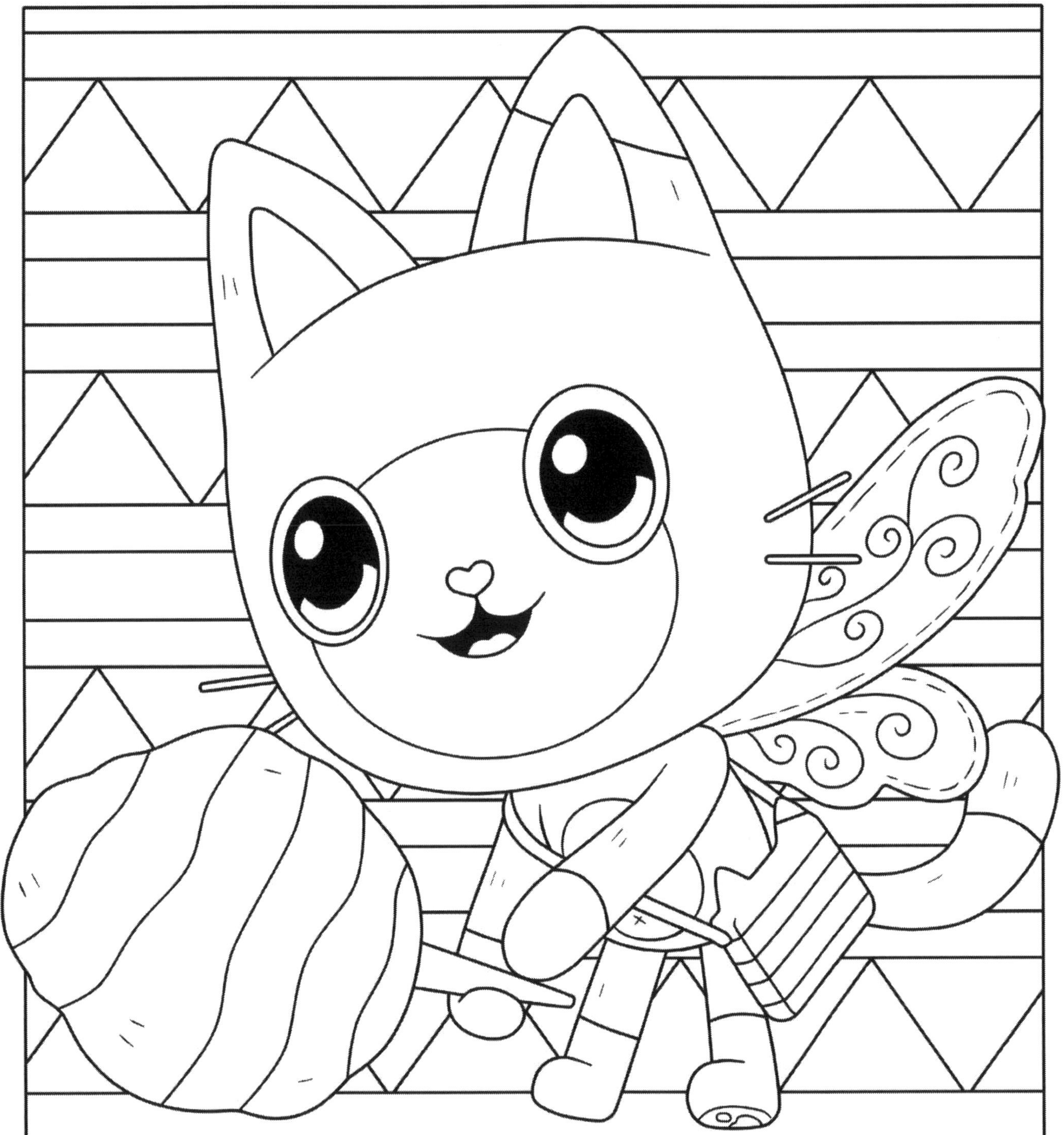

GABBY'S DOLLHOUSE

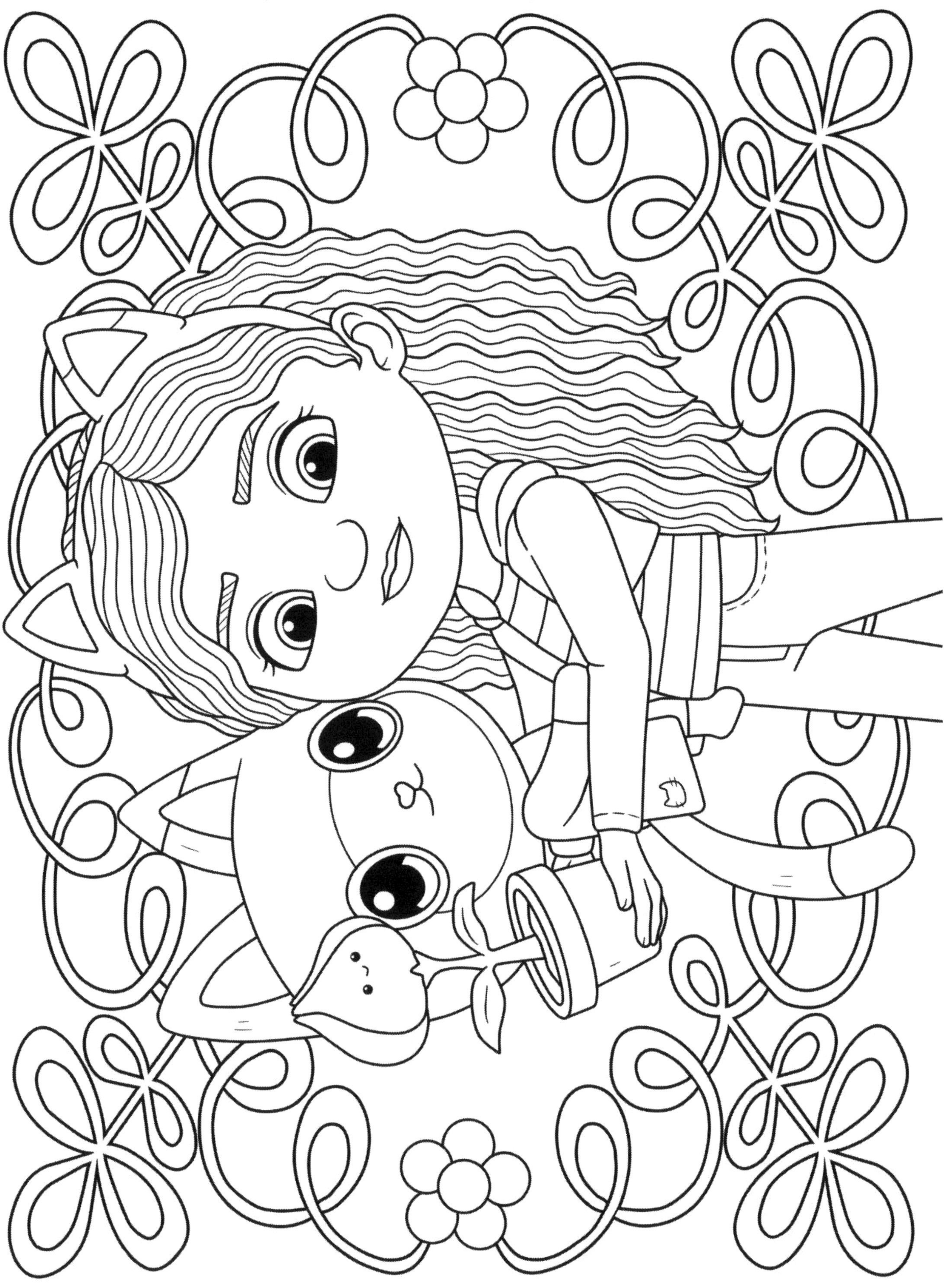

Printed in Great Britain
by Amazon

29769681R00042